we unknowingly create experiences we dislike. We blame the kitchen for the unsavory meals we are forced to eat because we have yet to learn that there is a cook in that kitchen, having his or her way with the meatloaf.

From cancer to jobs which burn us out, from money problems to unhappy love affairs, *As You Believe* presents a radically new and proven approach to personal problem solving. Based on the author's many years of experience as a psychic reader/healer, the book explains the inner processes which convert beliefs into events, details how to find the beliefs which are causing the negative experiences, and then describes exactly how to effectively heal for positive miracles.

This book answers the question: *Why do these things happen to ME???*

AS YOU BELIEVE

Books by Barbara Dewey

The Creating Cosmos
The Theory of Laminated Spacetime
As You Believe

As You Believe

by

Barbara Dewey

BARTHOLOMEW BOOKS
INVERNESS, CALIFORNIA
1985

Printed in the United States of America

This book is dedicated
to
everyone who is
courageous enough to change
his or her mind
about what life is or isn't.

Contents

1	PROMISES, PROMISES	1
2	THE CREATING COSMOS	4
3	POWERS OF THE MIND	11
4	AN OVERVIEW OF ENERGY MANAGEMENT	33
5	PURPOSE	37
6	AS YOU BELIEVE	42
7	THE CREATING MIND	54
8	EMOTION	70
9	THE PSYCHIC ENERGY FIELD	73
10	GAMES EGOS PLAY	81
11	MAKING OURSELVES WINNERS	88
12	WHAT TO DO ABOUT LOSING	101
13	ENDS AND MEANS	112
14	IN SEARCH OF CAUSE	120
15	BELIEFS WHICH UNDERMINE HEALTH	134
16	INTERPRETING PHYSICAL SYMPTOMS	152
17	HOW TO HEAL	181
	DESIDERATA	189
	INDEX	191

1.

Promises, Promises

DIANE AND I used to call it being hit with a blivy. Life, it seemed to us, was nothing so much as it was coping with the almost daily misfortunes of living. Together we were raising and supporting nine children, help from ex-husbands being problematical. Her boyfriend had a girlfriend, mine had a wife. Her children favored alcohol, mine street drugs. Her children preferred to stay home in sullen rebelliousness and get in trouble with the police. My children preferred to run away from home in angry rebelliousness and get in trouble with the police. The last time our lives touched, she had added a granddaughter to her list of dependents, had been butchered by a radical masectomy, and had put on fifty pounds. Thanks in large part to the path she had shown me, I was cleaning up my life.

Along with introducing me to the entire world of mysticism, psychic phenomena, and what is now called New Age Thought, Diane also lent me a very special book. It was called *Science of Mind,* by Ernest Holmes. "You will understand this even if I don't," she said. I understood it alright, but could I credit it? Holmes said that Mind created for the thinker whatever the thinker gave it to create. Negative thoughts produced negative events, positive thoughts produced positive events.

It was a very dismal suggestion! It implied that it was *I* who was the cause of my own misery instead of all those other people who were forever sticking it to me. Holmes was threatening the very foundations of my life—my innocence. I was, after all, the abused and it therefore followed that my misfortunes were someone else's fault. It was they who were wrong, not I.

On the other hand, if I had the kind of power which could create disasters, it also meant that I had the same kind of power to bring positive experiences into my life. I decided I didn't want to sacrifice my right to joy for the self-righteous pleasure of accusing others. But before I let go of all my pride I had to find out if what Holmes had to say was pragmatically true or if he were just speaking philosophically.

I began with small "healings"—dissolving headaches, finding a pet turtle or a convenient parking place—and worked up to more meaningful tasks as my incredulity turned to a conviction that Mind could, indeed *did,* create whatever it was commanded to create. I healed for big sums of money and money came pouring in. I healed for health and health returned. Eventually, I offered my services to others and the results were no less spectacular. In short, I became a psychic healer—and a committed believer!

In the intervening years I have worked my life around to where it is a pure, unadulterated joy. I couldn't be happier. By profession I am a psychic healer/reader though I seldom heal directly by removing symptoms. Instead I prefer to work with my clients to the point where they can do this for themselves. In the long run I do not think it serves a positive purpose to come off looking like Lady Whizzbang at the expense of the client's own self-image for we are all capable of effecting "miracles." My first promise, then, is that you will know how to create your own miracles by the end of this book.

As You Believe is more than this kind of icing on the cake. Miracles are fun but the greater miracle is a day-in-day-out blessedness and for that you need something more than showmanship. If your suffering is more than momentary, you need a basic re-ordering. So this book is also about how to change the structuring of your life at its *causal* level.

I spent a lot of years searching for the causes of my distress. I sometimes think the word WHY must be emblazoned permanently into my brain for no bout of tears was really done until I thought I had found their deeper causes. For many years my conclusions were totally wrong, but gifted with an ability to change my mind, I persevered until at last I began to get somewhere. Each of us must come to a truth in his or her own way. It would be nice to think, however, that I could make your own discovery process shorter than mine was. And so this book is also about the truths which I have discovered and which, in turn, may help you find yours.

The world is wiser than it was when I began my positive journey. There is a growing body of people committed to inner growth and expanding consciousness. They recognize that neither the materialism of science or the institutionalized religions of the West can offer sufficient promise to invite faith. But what *is* the greater cosmic purpose of life? Are we an evolutionary by-product of a Big Bang? Or are we here as God's children to be rewarded and punished as our conduct warrants?

These may sound like pretty academic questions, particularly in a practical how-to book, but without a context to give all acts meaning, all acts threaten to become meaningless. Well, I have something for you here, too. In my personal search for answers, I discovered, I believe, the truer design of the cosmos and hence the implied purpose of physical experience. I call the design the Creating Cosmos and it is enormously positive, enormously empowering, enormously caring. So not only will you have the intellectual pleasure of a deeper insight into the workings of the universe, you will also come away feeling vastly reassured. This book, then, is both a book about self-healing and a healing in itself. And that, too, is a promise!

2.

The Creating Cosmos

BEFORE WE GET TO the nuts and bolts of self-healing, I want to explain the cosmic mechanics which make such a phenomenon possible. As a culture we are so externally oriented that many will find unacceptable the concept of changing outer circumstances by internal means. That's because we haven't really known *how* our universe is created, myths about the Garden of Eden and a Big Bang to the contrary. I have a theory which supplies this missing piece of information. I call it *The Theory of Laminated Spacetime*. Its consequences for physics are discussed at length in my book of the same title. Additionally, the humanistic aspects of this theory are developed in a second book, *The Creating Cosmos*. Here we will restrain our remarks to a bare outline so that we can move ahead to our primary task.

I believe that spacetime (physical reality) is discontinuous. That is, there is a condition where everything exists followed by a condition where nothing exists, followed by a condition where everything exists once more. In the condition of existence we have limitation imposed by the dimensions of time and space. In the blank between the laminae of spacetime we have a *spaceless, timeless* condition capable of creating the entire cosmos in its next experience of space and time, and doing so eternally. That's a lot of

4

power! All of this happens so fast that we perceive the experience to be a continuum. Think of a movie film which is actually comprised of a series of still pictures but looks to be—when run at its proper speed—continuous action.

If this theory is fact, and it seems to prove itself out in physics by explaining the *causes* of gravity, polarity, weightlessness, etc., then we have decoded the Prime Creative Act itself. This creative act makes subjective reality the cause of physical reality. Physical reality becomes the effect of subjective reality.

To avoid buzz words, I have called this subjective reality the endosphere—the sphere within. By definition it is without the restrictions of space and time. By inference it is an undefined creating medium. I could have called the endosphere God, but our present concepts of God are so distorted that it would only detract from the majesty of the endosphere. I could have called the endosphere mind, but again, popular misconceptions diminish that word to meaninglessness. Mind, heavens forbid! is not the brain. The brain is a physical computer. I could have, most properly, called the endosphere energy—psychic energy—but here again popular concepts about energy as a physical component of space-time reality also present problems. The endosphere is *infinite power,* made momentarily finite by a creative process inherent within its own characteristics.

Everything which cannot be located physically is of the endosphere—the soul, consciousness, the psyche, etc. All properties which cannot be located physically are also of the endosphere—the emotions, personality, the will, the ego, etc. This means that all such qualities are timeless as well as spaceless. If you have ever fretted about your immortality, you can stop. Your body will come to its timely (!) end, but *you* are eternal—like it or not! Such a state of affairs is a great argument for getting on with the task of learning how to live positively. *Some*time, in *some* life you will have to learn how to handle life's grubbies. Why not now?

Because we are of the endosphere we are the same as God, if you will, but in finite form. Before this goes to your head, so is an ant and so is a leaf, and so is a pebble. They are all manifestations of the same "God-Stuff" and all therefore are divine.

We are not weaklings in need of protection. We have a super-abundance of power and can express our lives exactly as we wish. The choice is ours. We can understand ourselves to be powerful and divine creators or we can deny that responsibility as well as that power and call for a savior. We can behave as adults or as children. This freedom, too, has been granted. It means that if you ask for help in the right way, you will get it. But it also means you will continue to feel weak in comparison to your savior and delay the day of self-sufficiency.

We will address, very briefly, how something can be created from nothing but before we leave a description of how the cosmos is set up, I want to expand your perception of the design. I call the cosmos (All That Is) the Creating Cosmos because its design is in the service of the act of creation. The Creating Cosmos *is* energy, it is therefore an action. It is the verb *becoming*. It is not a thing, a noun, except as it momentarily shows itself in the illusion of its material form.

I describe the Creating Cosmos as the power, the purpose, the process, and the product. Again, the Creating Cosmos is All That Is. Between the blinks of laminated spacetime—as the endo-sphere—it manifests as the power and the purpose. The process is the definition and limitation of the infinite by spacetime. The uni-verse and all activity within it is the product. If we would describe any of this indivisible whole as divine, then we must describe all of it as divine. It belongs, in its entirety, to each of its physical mani-festations and each of its physical manifestations is 100% of itself. There is nothing apart from this condition of One. In spacetime, there is the illusion, but only the illusion, of separation and the concepts of cause and effect, beginning and ending, the dichotomy of good and evil, and the perception of lesser and greater creations.

At its most basic level, joyous living is the proper management of the creative energy of the endosphere. Through our minds we work with this creating energy to create whatever we wish. As long as we prefer pleasure over pain, however, it behooves us to manage this energy to serve that end.

One of the purposes of the Creating Cosmos is to make real physically what has already been made real on the subjective level. The process of mentally imagining automatically focuses psychic energy in direct proportion to the intensity of the imagination. When this focus of conviction or intention and its attendant psychic energy reaches what I call a state of critical mass it forms an I-am or statement of definition. I am an elm tree. I am a whale, I am a toe. I am a musical composition. I am a civil war. I am a dinner party. I am an atom. It is easiest to think of an I-am as creating an old-fashioned computer card for itself. This card is punched out in the design which describes that particular I-am or self. It is through this card that psychic energy must flow, like paints through a stencil, and when it does it creates a physical design by manifesting in space and time.

Selfhood, or an I-am, is very specific. It defines exactly what I am and what I am not. I am an oak tree, but I am not a canoe, or a picnic, or even an alder, a birch, or a pine. I am this particular oak, growing here in the particular clearing. I-ams cannot evolve, as Darwinists would wish, for the concept of selfhood cannot be supported and abrogated at the same time. An ape cannot evolve into a human because, if it could, the I-am of an ape could have no meaning. Without a specific symbolic intent it would lack sufficient definition to produce itself physically. It could not arrive at a state of critical mass. An I-am can only change within the workable extremes for that I-am because an I-am is an expression of a discrete idea.

Perhaps the most remarkable accomplishments of the Creating Cosmos is the phenomenon of selfhood and how it is managed. The cells within a finger have their own I-ams. The finger is an I-am within the I-am of an arm. The arm is an I-am within the I-am of a body. The personality of a particular body belongs to a larger gestalt of personalities, unseen, but undoubtedly intuited by those who have faith in a God. How many overriding gestalts abound in the great unknown world beyond our horizon, I cannot tell and it doesn't matter. They are we and we are they in the ultimate I-am of which we are an indivisible part. Reality is a system of wheels within wheels within wheels. The sum total is I-AM or ALL That Is or God—properly defined!

This is pretty phenomenal just as it is, but the truly remarkable part is this: each individual I-am is guaranteed the freedom to be itself, to be its own I-am, to the ultimate degree it can imagine for itself even as it is nourished, protected, and tended by larger and larger I-ams. In an age where too many of us feel isolated and unimportant, I think this is a valuable piece of information. The One is not a God; that One is indivisibly us in infinite form. Because of this, all I-ams are creating creations. They are simultaneously the product of their own creative efforts and the creations of larger gestalts.

The purpose of providing for a physical universe suggests itself, I believe. Within the true reality of the endosphere, cause and effect are one, there being no elapsed "time" between two events. This is not very instructive to practicing creators, particularly if we would like to awaken to our potential. Physical reality gives us the opportunity to experience our own creativity by living in the midst of what we collectively and individually have chosen to make real. Like it or not, we lie in the bed we have chosen to make. I don't suppose the Big I-AM really cares if we know this is happening or not—as long as it happens. But as humans, who prefer pleasure to pain, *we* might like to know. Physical reality gives us the slow-motion opportunity to discover what's causing our experience of life.

We, as humans, like to think in terms of right and wrong. We should have guessed—and in some ways we have—that any "moral" transgressions would be "punishable" according to law. It is inferred within the design of the Creating Cosmos that "moral wrong-doing" would be any negative thought patterns and that the punishment for that "sin" would be that we must live within the consequences of such thought patterns.

By accepting the conditions of physical reality we have also asked to live in the illusion of separation—from each other and from our source. Humans are probably the only I-ams who do not automatically feel a connection with All That Is and love themselves as part of that One. The illusion of separation not only symbolizes our self-doubt and alienation, it gives us a chance to work through the interior distress of various dichotomies by externalizing them. We see ourselves in others, hating in them what we hate in ourselves, loving in them what we love in ourselves. We contend with others because we are contending within ourselves. We punish and reward others as we would ourselves. The illusion of separation offers us the chance to resolve the interior inhibitions to unqualified love in a state of true union. Without this illusion and our reactions to other people, we might never even know such stresses existed.

The design of the Creating Cosmos infers that there are only two ethical commitments in the pursuit of a physical life. The first is to experience and express the soul-that-is-us as fully as possible. We are divine clay and it is up to each of us to cherish the responsibility we have chosen to undertake by making ourselves as grand a work of art as we can imagine. Such a commitment arises from self-love and self-respect. The first responsibility, then, is to love ourselves, tending the self as a divine gift to the world. Each of us should think of ourselves as a flower which we are expected to nourish into its blooming.

The second ethical law is to honor all creations as we should be honoring ourselves. The need of every manifestation should be equal in importance to our own. This does not prevent killing for food, for we are charged with our own care. But it certainly places an embargo on economic, social, political, scientific, and religious aggrandizement at the expense of other creations.

Thou shalt love thyself and thou shalt love others as thyself.

3.

Powers of the Mind

I F WE ARE GOING TO SOLVE our personal problems as well as our collective ones, we must first become familiar with the cause of those problems. This means that we must know every thing we can of the inner realm that I call the endosphere. We must know what it is, how it works, and how we can best use the system offered us to create what we wish rather than what we despair. Only yesterday, I saw a 23-year-old woman who was told only a few weeks ago that she will die of the cancer that inflicts her body. Fourteen years ago she began to build towards this cancer because she didn't understand the importance of inner reality and its causal relationship to physical reality. Yet this is but a single instance of the kind of sorrow we ignorantly create for ourselves.

Let's start this examination of inner reality by describing the endosphere as mind. There is no *generic* distinction between a mind which creates a solar system and a mind which invents the wheel. Everything which happens, happens because mind — a spaceless, timeless, creating medium — has been stimulated by a knowing thought to act out that thought.

What sets the "divine" expert apart from the human novice is the greater proficiency of the expert in the use of mind, his imaginative vision, and the greater amount of energy at his command. This is why I say we are so powerful. Potentially we have the power to create *anything*. We have the power of gods. It is therefore doubly tragic that we suffer feelings of frustration and impotence. These unfortunate feelings arise, not from any inherent inadequacy, but because we believe so profoundly in our impotence.

We did ourselves a great disservice when we externalized our own divinity and attributed all that was strong and powerful and good to a deity beyond self-identification. What was left—the fears, the weakness, the doubts, the guilts—we claimed for ourselves. Small wonder we feel so depleted, so incompetent!

Personal strength comes from self-confidence. Self-confidence comes from believing that we control our personal destiny and are not at the mercy of others. Personal destiny is created in the mind. The positive use of mind creates a positive destiny. The negative use of mind creates a negative destiny. It is as simple as that. Mastery of the use of mind so that we achieve beneficial results is the subject of the ensuing chapters. But, at the moment, I assume that most of you know far too little about the power of mind to trust such statements about mind's awesome ability. I therefore want to cite some examples of the use of mind in order to stretch your horizons beyond the limits of popular and disabling beliefs in man's general impotence.

*   *   *

Demonstrating the proper use of mind is not an easy task. We are kindergarteners all and there are no true examples of well-rounded adepts among us. We can only guess what the completed picture would be when we catch glimpses of it in one or another of us. But remember, what one man or woman can do, all men and women have the potential for doing.

I have devoted years to studying the power of mind and to using that power as frequently as I think to do so. From practical experience I can reach only one conclusion: mind can do any task we can set for it. It can literally create, destroy, and move mountains.

Through the proper use of mind we can have anything we want. We can achieve any outcome we wish. If the possibilities of mind lie dormant within most of us it is because we do not understand that mind is *the* creating force in all that we do and all that is done to us. If you are not experiencing the ecstasy that a proper use of this power brings, you have a Mercedes in your garage but think you must travel shank's mare.

Jesus said: "Ask and it shall be given you, seek and you shall receive, knock and it shall be opened to you." Like most of his statements, we have turned this invocation into a platitude concerning the spiritual rewards of a correctly pious attitude. This statement of Jesus is true. It should be taken at face value. It has nothing whatsoever to do with piety.

Mind is the creating medium used by consciousness, described here as an I-am. What an I-am construes its ability to be automatically becomes mind's tasks to fulfill. Mind easily performs its assigned tasks. What is not so easy is the expansion of human imagination to the point where mind can function as it is intended to function. The examples I give below should enable you to appreciate to a much fuller extent what mind *can* perform if it is given the opportunity by a willing consciousness.

* * *

Mind/consciousness is not bound by the fact or the laws of physical reality. Actually, it frequently finds physical existence pretty tedious and/or unpleasant. It will escape the body whenever it gets the chance or whenever things get a bit sticky because of emotional or physical pain. (This is why we faint; consciousness wants no part of the ongoing experience.) Whenever we are drugged, daydream, sleep, pass out, are anesthetized, or sufficiently traumatized, consciousness — and its mind — will leave the body. What this means is that all of us are naturally bi-local. Our bodies can be one place and awareness somewhere else. People who remember these occasions usually describe them something like this: "I was above the operating table watching the surgeons work on my body . . ." or "I was flying high over the town where I was born. I knew my body was in bed at home but . . ." This phenomenon is called astral travel and we all do this naturally. What is unusual is to remember consciously these experiences or even to precipitate them consciously and knowingly. Those who do so are using the power of the mind even if they do so accidentally. Mind is perfectly capable of total recall of all of its vast experiences — experiences which are far greater than one body and one life.

This means that we do not need elaborate and expensive vehicles in order to discover the truths of galactic space. We can travel through it astrally. Astral travel is very probably how the Egyptians obtained their astronomical information — information which astounds us, even today. Nor do we need to dissect the atom or perform exploratory surgery to discover facts. Mind is not limited by physical barriers. It can take us into the past or the future in the same way, for mind is no more bound by time than it is by space. Mind awaits only the appropriate demands made of it, demands which charge it with discovery.

Some minds can locate themselves physically in two (or more) widely separated places. Usually this happens when one of the bodies is asleep but adepts can be fully aware and visible in both locations. I once had a gardener who always brought his dog Chica with him when he came to work. He was here with Chica at the same time another customer — some 30 miles away — saw Chica sleeping under *her* tree. She specifically noted the time and date because she thought it odd to see the dog without her master and meant to account for it. If a "dumb" animal can do this, why not a sapient human?

Gravity can be overcome by the proper use of mind power. An object or a body can float free of support. This display is called levitation. Do the stories of flying carpets arise because our ancestors practiced this lost art? The phenomenon called poltergeist is a form of levitation, though its definition is usually limited to mean the events which take place in a room thus "bewitched." Objects in such a room slide back and forth in mid-air, crashing into each other or the walls. Commonly there is a teenager in the household thus afflicted. Do the powerful and often chaotic mental changes such a youngster undergoes during puberty trigger the release of mental capacities which ordinarily are suppressed by more controlled minds?

It is my own theory that the conscious use of levitation was used to build places like the pyramids and Stonehenge. To me, it seems much easier to get a master in the art of levitation to fly those massive blocks into place than to force thousands of slaves to tug and push them from God knows where. It also seems easier—and hence more likely—to shear those huge blocks to their precise measurements by using mind power—another level of expertise we will take up shortly. In any event we should not judge the gifts of others by our own insufficiencies. The art of levitation, through the power of the mind, remains a potential waiting only to be explored by the construction industry—or anyone else.

Mind/consciousness operates the body. It chooses birth and death and all circumstances in between. Doctors, however, tell us that health is as much an accident as disease. They maintain that the autonomic system which keeps the body functioning is beyond personal control. They describe this system as under the control of the computer brain and do not bother to ask what controls the brain.

Yogis, on the other hand, can consciously use mind power to control all vital functions. They can literally suspend all signs of life for weeks at a time. To all appearances—heartbeat, pulse, respiration, etc.—they are dead. One man[1] who was not a Yogi and who didn't know he could do this spontaneously, woke up in the morgue just minutes before his final disposition. That's how dead

[1]Joseph Chilton Pearce. *The Crack in the Cosmic Egg.* Pocket Books, 1971.

he appeared to be! After that experience he went on to earn his living for a time by consciously using his mind to control his vital signs. Yet doctors insist, and we keep believing, that the body functions on its own.

There is at least one man today who claims he has not eaten in 12 years. Through meditation—one method for directing the mind—he demands that his body be fed from the environment of air and sun. Apparently it is. Only when he must come to a city where the air is too foul to maintain health does he include a little lemon juice in his regimen.

Adepts can lie on beds of nails while they support heavy weights on their bodies. Yet they feel no pain nor suffer any puncture wounds. They can be stabbed with a knife and show no more than a drop of blood where the knife enters the body. I saw a film of a man whisking his hand through molten metal as it was poured from a vat. His hand was not even blistered.

There are entire tribes who use mental discipline to master the art of walking on red hot coals.[2] The art has become a form of initiation. The many who succeed do not even blister their feet. The few who have not engaged their minds properly die horrible deaths because the temperature of the coals is in the thousands of degrees. Adepts are even able to escort the uninitiated over the coals by holding on to them. This demonstrates the mental bonding which makes it possible for a healer to effect a cure in the body of another—an ability which is possible because we are of the spaceless endosphere.

Another tribe suspends its young men on meathooks and then swings them high overhead.[3] Apparently this practice originated as a test of a man's guilt or innocence. Initially no one survived, but there came a time when one man did. Now all participants manage this "miracle" and summary justice must seek satisfac-

[2]Joseph Chilton Pearce. op. cit.

[3]Joseph Chilton Pearce. op. cit.

tion elsewhere as the practice has now become a ritual to insure good crops. I avoid comment on the tribe's judicial system but the ability to survive trial-by-meathook again demonstrates what the mind can do if it is asked.

Carlos Casteneda describes all manner of "impossible" feats in his books. During his apprenticeship to the Yaqui sorcerer Don Juan, he learned how to run down a mountain at top speed in the dead of night, trusting his mind to properly direct his feet. Isn't that exactly what animals do? Do you think animals are smarter than we *could* be? Casteneda also learned how to throw "bands of energy" in front of him. He could then span chasms, leap trees and even mountains. I recognize that there has been much skepticism about these books from some quarters. In his defense I can only say that if levitation is possible, "throwing bands of energy" is only another description of the same phenomenon. I see no reason to doubt Casteneda. He doesn't threaten me.

Casteneda also reports seeing women, all pupils of Don Juan, running around the walls of a room, their bodies parallel to the floor—another form of levitation. One woman, a fat old squaw, became unrecognizably youthful and supple after undergoing Don Juan's rigorous mental and physical training. As aging seems to be our most feared biological process, perhaps this demonstration will help allay such a fear and re-inforce the notion that aging is neither inevitable or irreversible. Do you remember Jesus' statement, "As you believe, so shall it appear?" We get old because we believe in getting old. Showing age is as much a miracle of the mind as is remaining youthful.

If Don Juan's "bands of energy" intrigue you, you might like to introduce yourself to them with a small demonstration from one of the martial arts. It tests mental strength over physical strength and even contenders who are vastly out-matched physically can compete. Face to face, put your hand on your challenger's shoulder. Now, using only your physical strength, try to keep your arm rigid while he pulls down on your elbow with both hands. There is little contest. Your arm will bend. Your challenger, after all, is using both arms in a more advantageous position.

Now, imagine your arm is secured to a band of energy fixed to a point well beyond your challenger's back. As he tries to bend your arm, never doubt that the band of energy will support your arm as it rests on his shoulder, and *never* descend to pitting your physical strength against his. As long as you do not transfer your attention from mental power to physical power he will never be able to make your arm bend, no matter what his physical strength may be.

Ever so briefly I have tried to suggest a few directions in which a fuller use of mind can expand physical possibility. I do not imply that any of us can become instant adepts in any of these areas. On the other hand, I am certainly trying to underscore the potential which lies within each of us—a potential which is there simply because we have minds, minds which we are not fully using.

*   *   *

The Hindus have imaginatively invented a place where all the information of the universe is stored. They call it the Akashic Records. They have invented this place to reconcile the fact that all information is forever available with a human need made more comfortable by having such information in a physical location. The Hindus believe that if you imagine yourself knocking at the door of this library, you can receive any information you wish— past, present, or future—just as Jesus suggested. (Ask and it shall be given you.)

All knowledge is ours to have. My experience in the field of physics is a case in point. It would be nice to say that I simply consulted the Akashic Records, jotted down what I was told and then transcribed my notes. It was not that simple. Sometimes I took a whole day to unscramble a small point, but those points have confounded scientists for centuries. "Going to the Akashic Records" is a *mental* attitude—an attitude which says you *can* have the correct answers if you want them with sufficient perseverance.

Shafica Karagulla's book, *Breakthrough to Creativity,* [4] gives many, many examples of people using what she calls Higher Sense Perception or HSP. These people are "going to the Akashic Records" though they describe their methodology differently. One business man uses HSP to unscramble his corporation's problems. Mentally (psychically) he "looks in on" various plants and divisions to see if they are running properly. When he sees a problem, he deals with it through normal channels so as not to alarm his personnel because he frequently knows about their problems before they themselves do.

Another man, a doctor, "sees" psychically all the minute functions of the body and how they fit together. This tool enables him to make far better diagnoses and prescribe better therapy than he could otherwise. A doctor told me once that a study of autopsies at the Mayo Clinic revealed that doctors were right in their diagnoses only 50% of the time. Under these circumstances, I personally think doctors need *some* kind of help over and above technology.

Still others who use HSP attend "dream schools" night after night where they study their particular interests. This is only one more way of going to the Akashic Records.

If you enjoy gardening you should read about the Findhorn Community. [5] These people go to the Akashic Records too, although they call it speaking with the fairies involved. As a result they grew 42 pound cabbages, 9' foxgloves and strawberry plants which produced a pound of fruit a day. And they did it all in the northern reaches of Scotland where nothing much but foul weather grows on the windswept rocks and summer is very short.

It doesn't matter whether you believe your information is coming from the Akashic Records, from fairies, or from HSP. The point is that these are all examples of mind directed to find and retrieve information. Having been given that command, mind will

[4] DeVorss and Co., 1967.

[5] *The Findhorn Garden. The Findhorn Community.* Harper & Row, 1975.

find it for you. The source of this information does not have to be something esoteric like a fairy or a library in the sky or even psychic ability. A friend can come along and tell you what it is you want to know.

Mind can also perform astounding feats of memory and knowingness. Yet if we use mind as it is intended, we might not consider them amazing at all. Some people have "photographic memories." They can mentally flip through the pages of a book they've read and locate the specific information they want. They can then read the text verbatim.

Karagulla recalls a man who could read through an entire symphony once and duplicate it note for note. He could also do the same thing with a book of any size. The same man could also give the square root of a forty digit number faster than a computer could check his accuracy. The author, Truman Capote, could recall hours of conversation word for word. A waitress friend of mine who works in a posh restaurant where superlative service is *de rigeur* never writes an order down no matter how large the table. Once a diner said to her, "I'll have the vichyssoise and the name of your memory teacher!" When I asked her how she did it, she said, "If I *tried* to remember the orders I couldn't do it, but I can tell you right now what that man had for dinner." Perhaps she takes her orders the same way Casteneda runs downhill—simply trusting the mind to know.

Other people can receive full musical scores even though they have little musical background. Still others write or paint "automatically." Most of these people say that they are only the instruments of discarnate personalities who wish to demonstrate life after death. They may be right. On the other hand it is also possible that they are tapping into a greater, more expanded use of mind which feels so different they do not recognize themselves in this expanded dimension. It may not be a separate discarnate personality at all but a larger version of themselves expressing their own larger potential. Either way, it demonstrates another use of mind.

All minds can learn to read and understand the meaning of the written word at the rate of thousands of words a minute, given just a few weeks training. (300 to 500 words a minute is considered normal.) A system called Reading Dynamics has been success-fully teaching the technique for years. Yet, to my knowledge, all schools unswervingly agree that the only way to read is one word at a time. I ask you—is this attitude compatible with the computer age? No wonder we despair. We are being *programmed* to be dumber than our machines.

Transmediumism is another capacity of mind/consciousness. Some people with a particular kind of genetic make-up can vacate their bodies and allow another discarnate consciousness to take over. This transfer can happen intentionally or it can happen spontaneously. Some do not even know this has happened to them and go through life believing they are crazy. Sometimes they are locked away in institutions. A little gentle exorcism might end their misery and give them back their own self-dominion. Inci-dentally, exorcism—the act of driving out an unwanted spirit—should never be done by confrontation as is the popular belief of most exorcists and their public. A bothersome spirit is either troubled itself or inappropriately trying to help. It should there-fore be comforted and instructed, not challenged.

It is certainly wrong to infer that anyone who behaves irration-ally or has a "split personality" is a transmedium. It is far more likely that such a person is struggling with problems of guilt or self-hate. Furthermore, no discarnate can occupy a body without the tacit permission of the person owning the body. If mind/con-sciousness is too frequently away from the body, or if a personality believes ghosts are more powerful than humans, or a person feels psychologically weak, he could be inviting possession—though it does not follow necessarily. Mind, of course, is perfectly capable of protecting its territory against all comers if it is asked to do so.

Famous transmediums like Edgar Cayce and Jane Roberts have concentrated on bringing spiritual understanding and remedial advice to those who are interested. Both Cayce and Roberts, through their inner connections, seem to have tapped into a kind of omniscience which can treat warts and describe the Second Coming with equal ease. Yet I believe we do not need the intercession of another advanced personality to be privy to the same information if we wish it diligently enough and train our minds accordingly.

While it is the intent of both Cayce and Roberts to bring a larger spiritual perspective to our attention, their comments are alive with specific information. Seth, the personality who speaks through Jane Roberts, goes into some detail about the Passion Play we call the life of Jesus. He asserts that Jesus was not, in fact, crucified but that the supposed crucifixion nonetheless expresses with accuracy the drama we *wished* to experience. If Seth is right, this explains the reported after-death appearances of Jesus as well as his being "raised from the dead," doesn't it?

Edgar Cayce, on the other hand, outlined cures for many "incurable" diseases, gave "past-life readings" and stressed continually the relation of spiritual "dis-ease" to physical problems. He foretold the future and unravelled the past for those who asked for readings, though he frequently had no personal contact with them. Roberts' information is far more sophisticated than Cayce's. It is less personal and I think more beneficial, but you should investigate them both if you find transmediumism of interest. But beware! I have read books by others who also say they get their information from unimpeachable sources "beyond." I do not doubt they do, but being dead doesn't automatically bestow wisdom. If you thought Aunt Minnie a bag of wind when she was alive she very probably still is. Use your head (your mind!) in these matters. Many of these books are largely hogwash.

It is my belief that Leonardo Da Vinci was a transmedium. In no way do I mean to diminish his accomplishments. Transmediums are usually, perhaps always, in touch with another aspect of their own personality gestalt—a "past" or "future" personality linked to their own. Da Vinci, for me, only exemplifies the breadth of possibility open to someone once he removes the limitations of "I can't!" Those who paint or write or receive musical scores may also be transmediums; it's hard to tell. Whatever the case, mind and its capacities are being brought into play.

* * *

No one would deny how precious the sense of sight is, but mind has its own kind of sight and can "see" without eyes. There was a blind woman in Russia who could see color through her fingertips.[6] Others, blindfolded, can read books or describe pictures or other objects. Some people find that objects stimulate mind into knowingness. The art is called psychometry. Psychometrists see or know information by feeling a personal possession or perhaps a crystal.

There is also clairvoyance—sight on a mind level which permits the clairvoyant to go beneath the physical form and see the subjective or astral form and thereby diagnose problems on their originating level. Clairvoyants are not limited to that level alone. They frequently see scenes, faces, and the like. When I boil an egg I look inside to "see" if it is done to my liking and I suspect that all good cooks do this automatically, not even thinking of themselves as psychic.

These days the media are full of items about the talents of one sort of psychic or another. We seem intrigued by what others can do but are unwilling to consider we might have the same talents if we encouraged them. The range of psychic ability is so wide and the competency so varied that it is impossible to detail this talent. Some see the future, others relate details too intimate and too spe-

[6]Ostrander and Schroeder. *Psychic Discoveries Behind the Iron Curtain.* Bantam Books, 1971.

cific to be known by a stranger. Still others help the police to locate bodies or important clues. I know a woman, not a professional, who saw the details of a crime so clearly that when she related them to the police they threw her in the pokey as their prime suspect. To their way of thinking, she knew too much not to be directly involved. Many people suppress these talents to avoid just these kinds of circumstances. It is definitely not okay to be too smart in a culture which so strenuously denies mind its extended capacities.

Some psychics see their information, some hear it being told to them, some rely on knowingness—clairsentience. Some psychics are utterly astounding and others are largely frauds. We all have some psychic ability; use yours to tell the difference between the real article and the imposter.

Most families have their favorite stories of strange psychic experiences happening to one of their members. Sometimes a loved one "appears" at the moment of his death. Sometimes warning messages are received. Once I was silently stewing about my kitchen trying to find the egg beater. My 1½ year old—probably too young to know what the words "egg beater" would have meant had I spoken them—toddled over to the toy box, retrieved the egg beater, and silently handed it to me. Now! Why didn't *I* think to look in such an obvious place!

Some people almost always know who is on the phone before they pick it up. Others see or hear events before they happen. Others may inexplicably call a friend at the very moment they are truly needed. I know a woman who can grab out of nowhere the phone number where she can reach a friend even though the number is not her friend's or even a number she has ever used before. Another woman, who constantly has such experiences, took a most illogical route on her way to do errands. Just when she realized she was totally off course, she spied her son who had been involved in a minor auto accident—unharmed but in need of her help. Her psychic ability had guided her to where she was needed.

* * *

The human mind, like its big cousin divine mind, can create matter, it can destroy matter, and it can change matter. It exhibits, I believe, its most exciting aspect at this level of activity. There are those who can project their mental images so strongly that these images are picked up on film exactly as if they had used a camera to shoot the picture instead of their minds. Their minds behave exactly like light waves behave. I often wonder how much of this talent a gifted photographer knowingly or unknowingly possesses. Are his photographs "objective" or are his own thought waves mixed into the process?

I have seen photographs of fairies and gnomes taken by two little girls who said they played with the fairies all the time.[7] They were really trying to take pictures of themselves but the fairies kept getting in the way. The photographs, incidentally, were scientifically verified as to the impossibility of any tampering. I do not doubt they actually did see the fairies (no one probably bothered to tell them they couldn't). Because they saw them, they could photograph them, for the camera is only an extension of the person using the camera.

Using only the mind, there are those who can will objects to move, bend, or break. Others can control the flip of a coin with 100% success. I have a friend—a powerful psychic—who probably uses more energy thwarting her abilities than using them. Her experiences alone would fill a book. One kind of circumstance her friends have all become quite used to is her precognition of death.

Six months to two years before someone close to her dies, a "house thing" will happen. (Curiously, this is the timing between the initiating emotional trauma and the physical manifestation of some illnesses including cancer—of which more will be said later.) As an example of a "house thing," once a gum wrapper appeared

[7]Edward L. Gardner. *Fairies.* The Theosophical Publishing House.

on a newly made bed though no one in the household chewed gum. The brand name was Double Mint and the person who was to die was a twin. Another time she found her expensive jar of face cream with half its contents gouged out. She indignantly accused first her son and then her husband but they were as mystified and as innocent as she. "It was as if it had been violated," she said. The face cream had been a gift from a friend of hers who was to die some two years later from a particularly painful form of cancer. A third time a heavy ashtray cracked in two although no one touched it. She associated that ashtray with me, but we will delay an interpretation for the moment.

It was only after a half dozen such incidents that we began to draw connections between "house things" and death. For years she just thought of them as curious but meaningless. My own guess is that the distress she experiences (but doesn't acknowledge consciously because she cannot handle it) explodes. In other words, had she acknowledged this information and grieved or become alarmed or otherwise expended the energy which such information evoked, a "house thing" couldn't have happened. As it was, her energy created a symbol of what she was unwilling to consciously create. Yet, once again the *power* of mind is on display in both its ability to create and to destroy matter.

Several years ago I found two maple leaves, not indigenous to my area, in some very odd places. One was carefully centered on the seat of my car. The other was under a pile of junk where my friend Molly who creates "house things" had hidden my birthday present some years earlier. Both leaves were fresh, well into their fall coloring, which is not typical here in mid-August. They were also pressed flat as no leaf directly from a tree can be. I found the leaves on the anniversary of the day Molly had helped me move into my home. I wondered at the time if she had sent them but I didn't check it out because, as they say, we weren't on speaking terms at that moment. It was this rupture in our friendship which I believe was forecast by the cracked ash tray. By the time we reconciled, she no longer remembered any thoughts she might have had at the time—thoughts which might have sponsored such a creation.

She did remark, however, that she had begun collecting and pressing leaves similar to the ones I described. Because she deemed two such leaves "inappropriate to her purposes," she had thrown them out. Her comment intrigued me for we are life-long friends although our closeness is occasionally disrupted. I think both her love for me and her feelings of having discarded me would be heightened by an anniversary memorable for its closeness. It would therefore be so very accurate to send me her love through her discards.

Dowsing for water or minerals is another example of the power of mind. Skeptics usually explain the phenomenon as an electromagnetic sensitivity, though such an explanation only re-describes the puzzle, doesn't it? The dowser gets a freshly cut and forked stick which he holds in both hands with the stem end pointing away from himself. (My neighbor reported that he watched a dowser using a plain old plastic wand which worked just as well. So much for high romance!) When the dowser comes to underground water (or whatever he searches for) the pointing end of the stick is pulled to earth so hard that the dowser is literally powerless to restrain the pull. I've tried it and I know. Some dowse for water or other material by using a detailed map; they do not need to be physically present. Lost persons can also be found in this way.

Healing is another power of the mind. I have been consciously using the mind to heal for close to 20 years. Much of what I conclude about the power of mind is drawn from watching miracles occur. The example which is dearest to my heart is the spontaneous healing I did for my infant son. I say spontaneous because I knew nothing about healing at the time. It was only after I had studied the laws under which mind functions that I understood I had, in fact, performed a healing by the rules.

In foetal life, the blood circulation by-passes the lungs. With a baby's first breath, the opening between the two heart chambers closes, forcing the blood into the lungs. This didn't happen in my son's case. He was a very blue baby with a malfunctioning heart. By the time he was 4 days old he also had pneumonia. Two of his tiny ward mates had died of the same compounded problems in the few days he had been back in the hospital when the doctor tried to prepare me for the same eventuality. I went crazy. I returned to his crib, took him out from under the oxygen tent and shook him. Angrily I told him, like any mother frightened beyond reason, that he COULD NOT DO THIS TO ME! (Why this process works will be discussed in later chapters.) The next morning we took him home. Aside from a bit of a cough, he was a healthy baby.

On one occasion an inoperable cancer, gripping the aorta, vanished after a healing. There were even Before and After surgical operations to prove it. I saved someone else from a kidney operation. Because I never saw the man or got the details of his problem, I can only report what my mother-in-law told me. This was in the days when I naively volunteered my services without finding out first what was causing the problem or without involving the patient directly in his own healing. When my mother-in-law first called the man was in agony. He was scheduled to have an operation the next morning but when the next morning arrived all symptoms had vanished and the operation was cancelled. I now suspect it was a kidney stone. I have also healed venereal herpes for which there is supposedly no cure.

I helped another woman rid herself of an arm tumor. She had had a dozen or more operations for the same problem and, over the years, not only had her arm atrophied but the operations had made the situation so bad that the tumor was no longer considered operable. Once I found a goldfish belly-up in its tank; it was not moving. Within minutes after I began the healing process, it was swimming normally again.

These occasions stick in my mind because there is a certain drama about them. But I would remind you that *every* recovery you witness for yourself is a healing—a psychic healing—sponsored by the mind. And unfortunately, every illness you witness is a negative healing, also sponsored by the mind. No doctor can cure even the slightest scratch. That miracle is performed by the body properly directed by the mind. A doctor or other healer may assist in the process by restoring confidence to the point where the mind of the patient begins to think positively about getting well. Additionally, the physical symptoms created by the patient can frequently be ameliorated by the correct therapy. Yet again, if the therapy is accepted, it remains the mind/body which decides to accept it.

If the healings I can perform appear miraculous, it is because of the speed and ease with which they are accomplished and because the medical profession has labeled some conditions incurable. Incurable simply means that *doctors* cannot cure a particular problem. It is dangerous to assume that all possibility is limited to the medical profession's possibility.

There is also the field of psychic surgery. I'm sure there may be many quacks who claim to be psychic surgeons. They may indeed be in the greater preponderance. Nonetheless, I also believe that psychic surgery falls within the range of human potential. I therefore see no reason to doubt the likelihood that there are indeed some who can perform these skills.

As far as I understand the experience, flesh does not have its solidity at certain high psychic vibrational levels. Say that the molecules separate. Remember we do not find it mysterious when we can plunge our fingers into a block of ice once it has reached the vibrational level of water or steam. At this level, which is achieved by the surgeon through mental preparation, it becomes possible for him to insert his fingers into the body of a patient, perform the necessary manipulations, materialize and then extract some appropriately tangible symbol of the illness like a tobacco leaf or a chain, and finally finish up, leaving no outward sign of the "incision." The patient as in all cures would actually cure himself after he came to believe in his cure.

I saw one film, the purpose of which was to suggest how such an operation might be performed fraudulently — animal parts, capsules of blood punctured surreptitiously at the moment of incision, the concealment of fingers in such a way that they only looked as if they were entering the body, etc. It all sounded quite reasonable. But I have also talked to a couple who were free to take any movies they wished, some of which I saw. The wife had undergone psychic surgery. For what, I did not ask, but she described herself as cured. But the surgeon must have been up to something more than an attempt to perpetrate a fraud because he announced while exploring her abdominal cavity with his fingers that she was pregnant. It was something of a shock to the woman, but his diagnosis was later confirmed by more conventional methods when they got back to the States.

As you might expect, psychic surgery is illegal in this country. In part this is to protect patients from quackery. But quackery is usually defined as using skills doctors don't possess. If my friend can produce a leaf and I can produce a healing, why cannot an adept with these skills and more produce both with a little showmanship thrown in? You certainly do not need the surgery to produce a healing but you do need to convince a patient that something profound and meaningful is occurring or his own healing abilities will not be engaged. He will slough off the healing. Psychic surgery seems as dramatic and convincing a way as any I can imagine.

There was an amazing Pole[8] whom Stalin found particularly interesting because the man had predicted that if Hitler turned eastward he would lose the war. Among this man's many talents was his ability to exert his will (use the power of mind) to such an extent that, at Stalin's suggestion, he robbed a bank of 1,000,000 rubles merely by presenting himself silently to the cashier, hand-

[8]Joseph Chilton Pearce. op. cit.

ing him a blank piece of paper torn from a note book, and opening his attache case to receive the money. When the experiment was over and the money returned, the poor cashier had a non-fatal heart attack when he understood what he had been led to do.

This man, also at Stalin's suggestion, walked through ring after ring of guards to reach Stalin's inner sanctum without ever being questioned or, of course, without any credentials which would permit him to pass. He said he did all this by making others think or act as he wished. In this case he willed the guards to think of him as the head of police even though they were almost opposite one another in physical appearance. Once he escaped from a German detainment camp by willing his captors to abandon him simultaneously. He also rode free on trains by willing the conductors to accept a blank paper as his ticket.

From some now forgotten source I remember reading of another man who desperately needed a visa from a country which was not issuing them at the time. He decided to use positive thinking. All the bureaucrats he met with said, "No! Impossible!" and then proceeded to do exactly what was necessary to produce the forbidden visa without either argument or bribe.

*   *   *

As a culture we have not yet begun to use mind as it is intended. While the mind is not the brain, it is common knowledge that we use a relatively small portion of the brain. Estimates vary widely but ⅓ of its capacity is probably a high figure. The brain's huge untapped potential suggests to me that the wiring is already in place against the time we finally discover the inheritance that is truly ours and begin to use our minds as they are intended.

Were we to *set our minds to it,* I believe we could fly, we could live to be as old as Methuselah's 900 years in perfect health, we could run the half minute mile, we could know the truth on any subject and hence the solution to every problem. The meanest among us could be Mozarts and Da Vincis. We could control natural disasters and end the man-made ones of war, poverty, crime, disease, famine and injustice. We could enjoy vastly enriched lives free from fear and guilt. In short, we could begin to enjoy life on a plane which is now imagined only in fairy tales. The divine system is, I believe, begging us to do just that.

Ignorant of this innate power we have compensated for a perceived impotence by a massive technological build-up. Yet the less we can rely on ourselves, the weaker we will feel. Thus the solution has only increased the problem. The erosion of our power base through technology and the dimunition of self-respect which this erosion precipitates seems to increase geometrically. Look at us! We fear middle-age, sexual impotency, disease, our neighbors, the faceless criminal, the government, the other political party, other races, religions, nations, not to mention nuclear warfare. An arms build-up, crime, economic distress, and restricted civil rights are all symptomatic of a collective fear of personal impotence.

Those who feel strong in spirit neither fear their neighbors nor need to usurp advantage from them. They are sharers and co-operators. They dare to trust and are rewarded for that trust by fair dealings. Yet our government, acting in the name of the collective will, finds no crime too heinous, no intrigue too seamy if it is done in the name of national security. (National security is another way for saying "the pacification of national paranoia." And paranoia is the direct result of a perceived impotence.) The Home of the Brave (that used to be us!) proudly supports tyranny all over the world and commits itself to building all the war material it can choke down the throats of its customers. Individually, we live increasingly behind bolted doors, drugging our awareness by one means or another to keep reality at bay. Given the magnitude of our innate power this fear is at best ironical and at worst genocidal.

4.

An Overview of Energy Management

L IFE IS AN inner creative process outwardly expressed. Life is a *result.* There are two necessary components in any creative result—an idea or mental blueprint of what is to be created and the energy needed for its reproduction. Both of these requisites are of the endosphere. There is no difference in the creative process which produces a clay pot or a birthday party. The difference is in the blueprint and the raw materials chosen. Thus the external life we think of as real is only the display screen for the inner creative process. Only if changes are made at this causal level can the display screen show us something different.

For instance, if you are having one unfortunate affair after another, the solution is not to find yet another lover, hoping that this time it will be different, because it won't. Nor is the problem to be found in some personality trait or other surface characteristic of your love relationship. The problem lies within the manifold layers of your internal creating machinery where you have predetermined that your love affairs will be disasters. Therefore your luck will not change until you change the *cause* of your luck.

If we are to reorder our lives effectively we need to know three things—how this inner machinery works, how we mismanage it, and how to find the specific cause of a particular problem. We need to know how to read the symbols of physical reality (the dis-

33

play screen) correctly so that we can pin-point internal cause. We must be like auto mechanics, knowing that something is not working right in the motor itself, but picking up our clues to exactly what the problem is by the grumbly sounds the motor is making. The more familiar we are with the life process from its internal creation to its external manifestation, the better equipped we will be to make effective changes. In short, we must know ourselves— inside and out.

The sooner we understand that life management is energy management the quicker we can begin to manage life correctly. We deal with a highly responsive creative medium, obedient, like all energy, to its own laws. We must go beneath the inexact thinking of philosophy and psychology to a bedrock understanding of inner physics, if you will. We must think dispassionately of energy management.

Before we get into a detailed examination of the inner mechanics of the endospheric self, I want to give you a quick overview. I want you to see the forest before we begin to look at the trees. It may be foolhardy to attempt to compartmentalize an undifferentiated reality, but nonetheless I think it helpful to imagine a sequential series of events so that we, trained in linear thinking, can more easily grasp what is happening. Let's, then, invent a flow chart to simplify the simultaneous complexities of inner reality (See Fig. 1).

The will to live is emotional, but it is an emotion so deep, so undifferentiated that we cannot give it an adequate verbal description. Call it an innate yearning to exist in a state of becomingness. Call it a thirst to live. It is the compelling push behind the entire design of the Creating Cosmos. It is the command which forces us to keep the ball in play.

This yearning-to-be is filtered through belief systems which diffract its intensity into a personal picture of what life means to us in a display as individual as a finger print. Because beliefs direct the

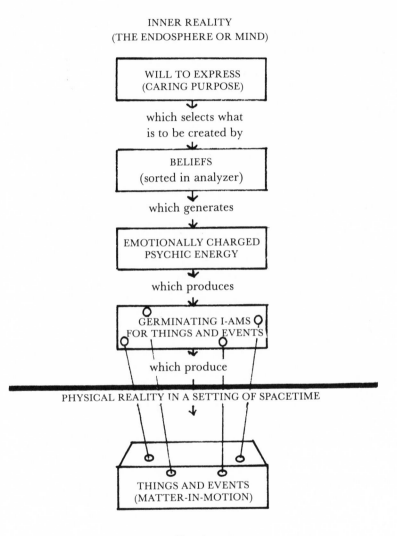

Fig. 1

power of creative yearning in a likeness of themselves, beliefs describe our interpretations of the life force. Beliefs are the blueprints for life. If you don't like some aspect of your life, you must find the offending blueprint-belief and correct it.

By the time the emotional base of the Creating Cosmos expresses itself in the emotions we understand—fear, joy, anxiety, love, etc.—the endospheric self is experiencing a reaction to its own belief system. In other words, an inner pattern throws its shadow on the screen. Our reaction to that shadow rebounds back upon itself to create an inner reaction. We cry because of a belief which makes us cry, not because of some external event. If you believe your kids should honor you on Mother's Day and they don't, you will cry *because of that belief*, not because of what they do. If you think Mother's Day is a scam, it wouldn't occur to you to cry.

Emotions are far more important than mere reactions, however. Emotions call up the amount and the kind of energy we will use to create physical experience. The greater the emotional reaction, the greater its creating capacities to compel a physical symbol of its characteristics. Therefore our reactions to life produces life. Physical reality is nothing but a reflecting mechanism. It is a backboard. It is a passive agent. It accepts what we create and bounces the consequences back for us to experience. Accusing life for our misfortunes is like accusing the television set for its rotten programming. If we are going to get better programs we will have to address our complaints to the broadcasting companies, not to the medium they choose for display.

Using the blueprints we have designed for ourselves in conjunction with psychic energy which is constantly pressing for expression, we create a "critical mass of intention" by steady emphasis. When it becomes real in the imagination, it *must* become real physically. And that's the story of your life!

Now let's look at this process in detail.

5.

Purpose

C OSMIC WILL demands that we persevere in our creative acts of becoming. We call this yearning for physical expression *the will to live*. When this deep subliminal drive wells up into consciousness where we can appreciate it in intellectual terms, we call this yearning, *having a purpose*. Purpose gives meaning to life. It *is* the meaning of life. When we use the very best of our abilities in the pursuit of a purpose we deem worthwhile we feel good about ourselves and about life. We are spiritually fit. We are in harmony with the creative intent of the cosmos and physical fitness necessarily follows.

The absence of sufficient purpose and its effects upon the will to live can be seen in the aberrational behavior of the captive gorilla. Female gorillas do not seem to have the slightest interest in tending their young, if indeed they can be induced to mate and carry a foetus to term. Zookeepers say this unmotherly behavior arises because these skills are not instinctive. New mothers, they say, must be taught these skills by watching other mothers. Because they live in adult troops without any babies these lessons are never learned.

What nonsense! Sex drives do not have to be taught! Neither does gestation! Furthermore, nurturing is the spontaneous act of love. It is far more likely that this freeze on maternal skills is the gorilla's way of demonstrating indifference to life as she experiences it. She has nothing to live *for*. There is insufficient purpose in her life to engage the will to live. Spoon-fed and carefully looked after, captive gorillas are denied even the simple dignity of participating in their own welfare. Without sufficient purpose to kindle the will to live, the gorilla's body is no longer "fit" to keep her kind going. Through indifference, she chooses death for the next generation as an act of compassion.

Humans and animals must feel the exhilaration of personal accomplishment. They must experience their own effectiveness— their personal ability to make a difference. Without an outlet to demonstrate such effectiveness, the will to live will be severely threatened. It makes me wonder how many laboratory animals die because they are held under conditions which defeat the will to live and how many die because the scientist in charge is killing them with his lethal doses of this and that. Be that as it may, for humans indifference to life is an alarm signal that something has gone wrong in the process of converting spiritual yearning into purpose. Welfare rolls, alcoholism, drug addiction, suicide rates, highway fatalities, the so-called breakdown of moral fiber—all attest to a society which, for too many, does not offer the means to a satisfactory expression of purpose.

The societal breakdown is largely due, I believe, to a state of transition in which we, as a culture, find ourselves. We move from 19th century purposes which are no longer relevant in the latter part of the 20th century, to 21st century purposes which are not yet in place. In other words, the guy who brought us to the dance is getting potted over by the punch bowl but we can't find anyone else to take us home.

Let me explain my point of view. The 60's were watershed years for us. During those years we witnessed the obvious failure of two time-proven life purposes which heretofore could be relied upon to give intense meaning to life. As yet we have found nothing to which we can dedicate our lives with the same enthusiasm. These were universal purposes which applied to all of us. Now we must find our own purposes and this is not nearly as easy as having purpose thrust upon us.

The first purpose which lost its compelling power to absorb our attention and provide a meaningful and socially unified focus was war. Because of the atomic bomb, war is no longer a life/death threat of heroics in which we can throw ourselves with enthusiastic and self-righteous purpose. The second purpose which went by the boards was the life/death challenge to survive. By survive, I mean a food-on-the-table-roof-over-the-head sort of thing. Survival became a part-time job and if we had a full-time job, it meant luxuries, not necessities. As a matter of fact, we no longer need to look to our survival at all. We can become captive gorillas and the state will take care of us.

Before the end of World War II, war was a do-or-die endeavor wrapped in the patriotic emotionalism of Right Action. War was the unquestioned and proper means of acting undividedly in one's own self-interest. Besides, it was publicly approved, nay, demanded, and it is always a great comfort to have individual purpose publicly supported. Unless one disagreed with the concept of war, war guaranteed the opportunity to make life meaningful and win self and societal approval all at the same time. With the advent of the atom bomb, however, war is neither a sane choice nor is there likely to be much opportunity for personal involvement. What used to come to every generation as a ready-made purpose for living (or dying) has been denied to us. While the sacrifices of war are being asked of us (taxes, depletion of non-renewable resources, peace of mind, etc.) we are forbidden the psychological stimulation of an opportunity for working in the service of a great, culturally supported purpose.

Before World War II, keeping body and soul together demanded the best efforts of both. Recently, I discovered among my father's papers a doctor's bill from the early 30's. It was for $65 — the charge for setting my broken arm. It was an exorbitant fee for those times. A country doctor was to set the same arm 2 years later for $15. But what made the bill so poignant for me was that in spite of the fact that we lived comfortably, my father had found it necessary to pay the bill in $5 installments. As our black Bessie earned a dollar a day when she was lucky enough to find employment, it is impossible to imagine what she would have done about such a bill for there were no welfare safety nets for anyone. You lived by your wits or perished. It was a deplorable and cruel situation for all but the wealthy. Nonetheless, living on the thin edge between life and death provides a focus for endeavor which can be found nowhere else except on the battlefield.

Denied the traditional opportunities for making life meaningful, we are being forced to find meaning elsewhere. This may demand a certain amount of conscious and dedicated effort, particularly as a high-tech society like ours is hell-bent on raising the standard of living by lowering the quality of life. Too many of us are captive gorillas with two cars, a dishwasher, and a job which deprives us of any sense of real purpose. Thus deprived we are apt to look to our personal relationships to give meaning to life and to bolster our sense of worth. It's about the biggest mistake we can make. Relationships can fulfill the wish for intimacy and caring and partnership but they cannot supply the missing feeling of self-worth. The high divorce rate is a cultural phenomenon bred of our attempts to do this.

Purpose must be expressed in effort—the more the better. Someone who has properly engaged him or herself in the process of life works hard at everything he does. He plays (or goofs off) just as vigorously. He sets outrageous goals for the fun of it. He welcomes new challenges. He is alive. He is turned on to life. He is enormously rewarding to be with. He knows you do not pursue happiness. Happiness is the by-product of a life spent in the pursuit of worthwhile purposes. If I haven't just described you, you are plugging through life without sufficient purpose. It's a good bet that you are waiting for the Sugar Fairy to *make* you happy. "I only want to be happy and that would happen if I had a boy friend/baby/new house/different job/rich uncle." It doesn't work that way. Life is only what you think it is. If the Sugar Fairy did drop by, before she could open her mouth you would zip out your spray paint and color her gray so she would look like what you were expecting.

I think the cosmos is trying very hard to get this message across: "It doesn't matter what you do as long as you do it with gusto. The greater the challenge, the more exhilarating the experience. No one loses who plays this game. No one wins who doesn't."

6.

As You Believe . . .

W E HAVE LITTLE of the instinctual mental patterning which directs animal survival. Without the benefit of such automatic behavior, we must build our own rules to guide our actions. Mind makes up these rules for us by constructing belief systems from the information we take in through experience. Belief systems give structure and meaning to what would otherwise be chaos.

But meaning for us implies evaluation and evaluation brings with it the concepts of right and wrong. This makes human awareness much more complicated than animal awareness. Only very occasionally must we cope with the biological distinction between fight or flight. On the other hand, we must continually cope with the reasoned distinction between alternatives. All this extra work is the cost of the privileges we enjoy because of our expanded use of mind. Belief systems are for humans what instincts are for animals.

Belief systems provide the same safe passage through our subjective experiences of life that biological "instincts" provide our bodies. In theory, this refinement of an instinctual system should work well, but in practice it may prove self-defeating, for, as we shall see, we are hog-tied by our belief systems.

Beliefs do, however, have one redeeming feature which instincts do not have. They can be remodelled, exchanged, or abandoned as often as we wish and we are therefore always free to start afresh. Because belief systems can be lifetime masters and because we cannot change the patterns of our lives until we change our beliefs, it is vital to understand the importance of beliefs.

Our introduction to the use of mind and our reliance upon its abilities may even start before birth, for the human foetus has a dangerously long umbilical cord. It can wrap around a foetus and strangle it. Every other animal I know about (with the exception of the gorilla) has a stubby little cord, so it isn't as if a better adaptation hadn't been devised. Why is it that humans—the supposed *piece de resistance* of the evolutionary process—are subjected to such arrangements?

One possible answer is that the foetus is being forced into high gear because it is being coerced to use its mind to solve its problems instead of trusting to physical instincts. If this is true, then the intrauterine experience is an unforgettable one, for with nature's appalling economy when she selects that route, the umbilical cord is at once the life force and the death threat. The cord is essential to the survival of the foetus and yet it is also capable of killing it. Under such conditions the foetus has no alternative but to begin to learn the art of using its wits or suffer the consequences. So, just as the first tap on a baby's bottom induces breathing, the umbilical cord may be the first threat to survival which forces experimental learning and the subsequent fervor for guidance systems.

Mind/consciousness has an analyzer. Although it is, of course, not physical, I like to think of it as a computer with a multiple number of responsibilities. It processes all incoming data in such a way as to give that data meaning. Such incoming data includes not only direct experience, but the input from books, teachers, the media, dream experience, wild imaginings, and the idle thought. The analyzer is a reference library catalogued for ready use.

It is to the analyzer we go for guidance every time we make even the smallest decision. In order to be useful the analyzer must be incredibly efficient in coming up with the appropriate directions we demand of it. It must be ready with "automatic" guidance. To serve this end, the analyzer doesn't much care for odd bits of meaningless information. It prefers the more simplistic (and faster) approach of building choice-makers, or belief systems, which can describe truth cleanly—right on one side and wrong on the other. With such belief systems in place, it can then process incoming data with greater efficiency, giving it its proper value, storing it under the appropriate headings, etc. And it can just as efficiently give the proper orders as occasion demands.

All in-coming data is stored in the analyzer under the appropriate headings as pictures. Unlike snapshots, however, these pictures have been tampered with. Before they are accepted by the analyzer, they have been colored with the emotional feelings and subjective evaluations of the ego. They are distorted, censored, edited, and exploited to fit the pre-conceptions of the ego and the ego's idea of what the picture *should* look like.

In effect, this means that all incoming data is more than likely to be tailored to fit what biased information is already in the analyzer or what has been already approved by the ego. ("She's wearing red, my favorite color. My! She's so well dressed.") The result is that the ego simultaneously creates and takes orders from a system which it has designed all by itself. Thus it goes to an oracle in search of truth so that it may be well guided, and it hears only its own voice. Such an arrangement would be seriously flawed if objective truth were the goal of life. But it isn't. We are asked only to live in our own truths as we have devised them. Therefore we who have made the rules must be bound by the rules we have chosen to make.

Because each of us is guided by individually designed guidance systems, no two people will ever experience the same occasion in the same way for the information is being edited by our analyzers even as it is being experienced. One person's analyzer causes that person to notice the flower vendor's stall and the little bird bathing in the gutter. Another's analyzer tells that person to see the brooding skies, the tense and hunched bodies of the passers-by. Consequently, when the scene is duly recorded as "fact," the truth about the scene has already been distorted. We can, therefore, never perceive what is real. We can only perceive what is real for us.

Experience is so strongly warped by the person undergoing the experience that I used to wonder if "out there" were nothing more than a blank screen upon which we projected our own cinematic versions of a three-dimensional movie. It is a bit more complicated than this because "out there" is interacting with each of us. But the truth is that we do create our own reality and the simile remains useful. What's more, such an idea suggests the reason why we can feel so isolated as we experience life from our own little projection booths.

One important piece of business for the ego is to manage its own comfort and, perhaps more than anything else, the ego seems to fear the isolation which subjectivity risks. It wants the assurances that collective agreement brings to subjective impressions. ("Did you hear that noise?" "Was he insulting me or am I reading something into his behavior?") "Am I crazy?" is never too far from the top of the ego's question list. It seems to know how terribly plastic reality is. To give that reality the appearance of stability, the ego goes to great lengths to find agreement with other egos as to what is so and what is not so. Facts, or the *sense* of objectivity, are only found in agreement with others and in *no other way*. Scientists, for instance, are in the business of finding agreement so that they can produce the facts they wish to produce. They do not "find" facts; they create them. Then, to make their creations "real," they find agreement. Such is the task of the ego also.

The material from which we construct our belief systems comes to us in two ways. Either that material is based on direct experience (by far the more compelling alternative) or it is based on the experience of others. In our society, this kind of secondhand information is a much more preponderant source of "truth." Do you really know, for instance, that Columbus—or anyone else—discovered America? That hydrogen atoms combine with an oxygen atom to form water? That the Russians wish to destroy our way of life? That carcinogens cause cancer? That sugar has no health value?

Most of what each of us thinks he knows to be true is taken as an act of unquestioned faith in someone else's wisdom. It is a shorthand substitute for direct experience. There is nothing wrong with this; indeed, it is necessary if we are to advance civilization. But it does not hurt to remember that such trust is not always warranted.

The process of maturation is primarily the process of discovering what "facts" a particular society agrees are acceptable or unacceptable. From the moment a child is born, his parents gently but persistently direct him to accept some impressions and reject others. His more honest and intuitively understood perception of a kaleidoscopic and unstable reality is slowly focused on one acceptable reality which agrees with his parents' reality.

Schooling continues the process of a child's societal indoctrination, bringing a particular system of facts and cultural beliefs to the attention of the students. Such indoctrination is even more important in a democracy because the effectiveness of such a government rests primarily on consensus and only secondarily on force. For instance, until a people all believe in majority rule, that majority cannot rule unhindered. Our obsessive wish to see democracy spread doesn't seem to take this into account. We think democracy rests on open elections and it doesn't. It rests on a cultural agreement that winners rule.

The course of our lives is determined by a series of decisions which set action in motion. The sum of these decisions describe our personal and collective histories. All decisions are directed by the analyzer and thus the analyzer chooses the events we call our history. A decision to act can be anything from a job choice or marriage to the so-called automatic functions of the body which keep physical life going. If life is expressing itself in self-defeating or unsatisfactory ways, then we must look to the analyzer and its belief systems in order to find both the problem and the solution. Therefore, knowing exactly what is happening within the analyzer can be of great benefit.

All incoming data is filed under four principle headings: Forget, Remember, Emphasize, and Suppress. It is the self, guided by its ego-aspect, which decides what belongs where.

Most of our experiences are filed under Forget—the scenery by the side of the road, the date Louis XI ascended the throne, perhaps your spouse's birthday (alas!). The analyzer receives the information but the ego chooses not to mark it. It does not think of it as significant. Unmarked, the pictures are there but they carry insufficient emotional coloring to be retrievable or remembered under ordinary circumstances.

Much of our experience, of course, is remembered. For reasons of its own, the ego cares enough to take note and so to imprint the material. This material is usually of a benign nature, noteworthy, but of passing interest—what you had for breakfast yesterday, when you must pay your taxes, the "facts" and figures which support your current truths, the more unusual events which make up your life, etc. Beliefs are not likely to arise from this category, although this material is apt to support beliefs. Beliefs can subsequently change the material in this category for none of the material in the analyzer is dead. It is always alive and potentially vital. It can be, and is, constantly re-worked and re-colored.

The third category—certainly the most interesting from the point of view of understanding beliefs—is the one labelled Emphasize. It is here that beliefs are most likely to be created. Here the pictures are highly charged with emotion and the emotion is likely to be some form of fear. These pictures represent danger points for us and we energize them accordingly. It is around these areas of distress that we wish to build our "survival" techniques, for we wish most fervently to avoid pain (physical and emotional). Energized, these kinds of pictures act like selective lightning rods. They attract other similar pictures to themselves and repel opposing pictures. This kind of selectivity can soon build up a sort of castle of nearly impregnable proportions. We grow prejudiced. We develop beliefs. We make systems from these beliefs.

Reports on the dangers of smoking, the fate of cancer victims, the Soviet Union's malevolent intent, etc., are taken on so readily as unquestioned truths because the emotion such reports arouse is fear, and fear will mark well the path of deliverance from any imagined harm. We are far more ready to accept a fact which scares us because we don't want to be hurt. We mean to jump to safety if we can.

By far the most devilish category under which the analyzer stores its data is Suppress. We do not forget the pictures filed here. On the contrary, they are so highly charged and so unacceptable that the only way the ego knows how to deal with experiences it can't forget and won't remember is to cover them up with a pleasing picture of an opposite nature. The effect of this cover-up is like living with a pressure cooker. The "good" covering picture must work doubly hard to keep the "bad" (and charged) picture from escaping into conscious awareness.

Most of our common emotional problems arise from this category and the phenomenon will therefore be discussed in a later chapter. It is enough to say at the moment that these unacceptable pictures create opposing beliefs which are the strongest of any of our beliefs. They have to be. They are working double time. Such pictures can be inferred in the behavior of the super-courageous (a fear of cowardliness), the super-good (a fear of their own "evil") or the super-sexual (a fear of sexual impotence), etc. What these people are doing is covering a feared truth (picture) with a covering truth (picture) which denies what is feared. It is uphill work. It demands the dedication of a zealot to keep the covering picture in place.

* * *

Well! How does all this acquired information translate itself into action? Let's imagine that you have just seen a dog and you decide to acknowledge this fact and not simply to file it under Forget. Your present picture catalogue may allow you to know that it is big and black. That is, you may have been sufficiently indoctrinated to agree on what big and black signify. If you have a greater assortment of pictures, you may be able to identify the dog as a poodle. Again, *dog, big, black,* and *poodle* are all generally accepted social agreements as to "facts." Now you specific set of pictures and the beliefs you have created from them begin to come into play. The conversation you have with your analyzer might go something like this:

You: Something is coming towards me. What is it?

Analyzer: (matching the picture of what is happening to what is already in the file) It's a big black poodle. You don't like dogs. They bite.

You: This one seems friendly enough.

Analyzer: (sorting through dog pictures, all of which are colored with some fear) No! Don't take any chances. You are really afraid. The dog will probably bite you.

You: Then I'm in a jam. What shall I do?

Analyzer: (consulting success pictures) Do you remember the time you thought your mother had caught you sneaking cookies? You were in a jam then, too, but you pretended that you were innocent. That is what you should do now. Stand still and pretend you are not afraid of him and maybe he'll go away.

Notice how the analyzer switches from the subject at hand (a

dog) to an incident involving your mother. The analyzer is looking for something which might offer guidance and will attempt to
match your current need with any useful information. Story lines
are not important. What matters is the emotion behind the story
and the kind of identification which is made by identical emotions.
In this case, fear of an authoritative figure is binding the present
incident to the past incident. Furthermore, the cookie incident
was stored as a success picture with the annotation, "If I ever get
into trouble, I can bluff my way out of it." This picture is thus
available for ready use should it ever be needed.

If the present dog is properly fooled by your bluff (or had no
intentions of biting in the first place) you will file both pictures
together and one will reinforce the other. You will now have two
success pictures, which are "the same"—the same in terms of
feelings generated. You may be well on your way to having a belief that bluffing is a good way to get out of a tight spot. The next
time you meet a dog (or a mugger or a cop with his red light flash-
ing or an angry mate) your analyzer will instantly be ready to shoot
back the command to freeze and appear guileless. It will no longer
have to go through all the sorting process it went through with the
dog. The appropriate response has already been decided by a belief and you can now perform automatically, "instinctively."

On the other hand, if your bluff fails and the dog menaces you,
the analyzer may add a notation to the cookie picture. "This
doesn't work on dogs and maybe it was just dumb luck that made
it work on mothers." Again, it may file the current dog picture in
such a way that it becomes the basis for a brand new belief that
running from a dog is the better part of wisdom. If trauma warrants it—if the dog bites, for instance—a new belief may become
crystallized right then and there. "Run like hell from anything
which menaces you—muggers, cops, mates, and mothers included." Yes, such a traumatic experience can re-color all previous success pictures so that your belief in bluffing may become

so weakened that you abandon it altogether. If you are lucky, that is. It is perfectly possible that both beliefs will be sufficiently strong that your analyzer will direct you to stand still and run at the same time, for such are the problems with a system like this.

It should be underscored that everyone who encounters the dog will have his own experience with him. Some will find the dog friendly, others will not even notice him. Even if everyone else sees fit to stand still, their reasons for doing so will all be somewhat different.

I cannot stress strongly enough the extent to which our beliefs determine the course and content of our lives. The analyzer, armed with those beliefs, tells us when to be afraid, when to feel hurt, jealous, aggressive, sexual, or happy. Beliefs tell us when to snatch an opportunity and when to ignore one. Beliefs do more than that, of course. Beliefs create opportunity as well as withhold it, as we shall see in the next chapter.

Beliefs determine our eating habits, our health record, our work attitudes, whom to follow, whom to love, whom to fear. Our belief systems establish our expectations for ourself and others. Our self-image is fashioned from beliefs. Beliefs catalogue our likes and dislikes, our truths and falsehoods.

We hold beliefs on every facet of life—ethics, religion, politics, sexual preferences, obligations, artistic taste. Our beliefs are what determine the prospects for life itself. Will life be a raw deal beset with poverty and misfortune or will life reward our efforts with lots of good luck? Will we be loved or rejected? Happy or miserable? Comforted or abandoned? Successful or disappointed? All these possibilities are determined by our beliefs because beliefs force their own reality. We can choose whatever reality we wish. We can (and do) write our own scripts by the simple mechanism of holding beliefs. If your life is less than ideal, it is your beliefs which are creating this. Properly, you can never blame it on circumstance.

Because beliefs are our truths we cannot disobey them. Those beliefs that describe morality coerce through guilt. Those that describe limitation coerce through imagination. Those that describe truth coerce because we think of them as fact. We are either unwilling or unable to set a course counter to our truths.

No one can make the statement that belief systems are necessarily logical, well reasoned, or indeed, that they abet right choice, though this is the intent behind their creation. Neither are they built on truth. In the 14th century, it was a fact that the world was flat. It was believed by everyone with as much conviction as we now believe that the world is round. It is very important to recognize this because if we wish to change a belief it is much easier if we understand that *all beliefs* are only opinions. We do not deal with facts—*ever!* We deal with beliefs about what facts are.

From the point of view of those who think that perseverence will bring them to the safe harbor of their own infallibility, it is unfortunate but we are at liberty to build belief systems any way we wish, given the freedom we enjoy. There is only one rule: each of us must sleep in the bed he or she makes. Were I in charge of the universe, I could not summon the courage necessary to permit this kind of freedom. I would be cowering in the passenger's seat the way I did when I taught my oldest son to drive. Trusting him with the freedom to kill us both so unsettled me, my next four children had to find other instructors. But Somebody Up There seems to have a faith that everything will eventually work out for the best. That faith should quicken our gratitude as well as our best efforts, for that freedom is more precious than all else.

We are slaves to our beliefs. It is therefore up to each of us to choose better masters if we want richer, more rewarding lives. There is nothing in the nature of a belief itself which makes it sacrosanct. Beliefs get stuck because we have come to *believe so much* in a particular belief that we cannot see that it could be other than the truth. It is our faith in our beliefs which makes them so difficult to alter. How beliefs can be changed will be discussed in Chapter 14, but until we make those changes we will never be able to escape the effects of the negative beliefs we hold. We are doomed to all the bad luck they create for us.

Each of us wants to be good. It is natural to be good and to this end we struggle—sometimes with results so bizarre that they would seem to contradict such a statement. We yearn for truth. We truly want to know the right of the matter and it is towards this end that we strive—hopefully, tirelessly, and, I think, courageously. If we fail, it is because we do not have sufficient information to make correct judgments.

If for no other reason, humans should be loved and admired for the tenacity and guts they display in trying to make the good life come true in spite of all the grief they create and endure in that very cause. Life does not cause pain. Life is only a reflection of what we believe it should be. It is our beliefs about life which cause pain. But beliefs can be changed and therein lies our real hope.

7.

The Creating Mind

WE BEGIN NOW an investigation of the mind's creative process, and therefore a quick review of the Creating Cosmos is in order. All forms of consciousness—organic and inorganic—are comfortably supported by the timeless, spaceless endosphere. Consciousness does not blink off and on. Physical form blinks off and on. Consciousness, or an I-am, determines its own physical manifestation and defines the form that manifestation will take. More preponderantly, consciousness, or an I-am, defines what it is not.

We call our particular form of consciousness *mind* and we call our individualized selves, I's. Although human creativity is far more profound than man's ability to imagine and build a cathedral or devise and operate a torture chamber, these illustrations suggest the difference in creative ability between ourselves and the animal kingdom.

Life, as we experience it, proceeds in a series of events. By event, I mean anything which can happen—the creation of matter, birth, a chance meeting, the orbit of the earth around the sun, the eruption of a volcano, puberty, falling in love, a nuclear war, the beat of a heart, the bloom of a flower, the cohesion of hydrogen atoms and oxygen atoms. Thus if we are to understand our personal histories we must understand how an event is created.

54

Psychic energy produces all that is. Like it or not, we are forced along our paths by pulses of psychic energy. Our hearts beat, our lungs fill and empty, we age, we work and play, all because we are under the continual command to become (something different) if we are to exist at all. We cannot escape using psychic energy and therefore we cannot escape taking an action. We have then absolutely no choice as to whether or not we wish to use psychic energy. We can only decide if we wish to use it consciously in ways that bring us satisfaction or continue using it in ignorance and risk the misfortune which so patently describes so much of the human condition.

Psychic energy obeys laws as precise in their effect on human events as is their effect on electricity or gravity. If the world seems chaotic and haphazard at the human level it is because we do not understand the laws which rule our personal and collective histories. Chance does not cause the moon to orbit the earth. Nor does chance make you the victim of a mugging. The misunderstanding comes from the fact that one phenomenon has been explained, more or less to your satisfaction, and the other has not. And it is this omission I would like to correct.

Psychic energy is directed by mind/consciousness to manifest as matter-in-motion. Mind/consciousness is a defining agent which sets off the use of psychic energy. With the determination of sperm and the opportunity of seeds, thoughts will always attempt to recreate a description of themselves in physical reality. Psychic energy can therefore be a very dangerous medium. Few of us understand that we play with very potent stuff by thinking it into existence. Jesus said, "As thou hast believeth, so shall it be done to thee," but no one took him with the seriousness which should have been accorded his wisdom. Unfortunately most of us think those words mean something like, "If you put on rose colored glasses a grey world will seem a little less drab." Not so. It means you are sentenced to live in the stage play of your beliefs.

While a fleeting thought is not apt to manifest psychically—call it a seed which didn't find a fertile environment—thoughts which carry sufficient intent *will* reproduce themselves. Thoughts which carry emotional impact, thoughts which are constantly repeated, thoughts which are beliefs and carry the conviction of truth are all the kinds of thoughts which are sufficiently stimulating to effect a materialization. If you imagine thoughts to be like seeds, then those which are provided for by repeated and proper nourishment are the ones most likely to produce a garden.

*   *   *

In addition to the knowledge that our minds sponsor all creative thought and therefore produce all our life-experiences, there are three characteristics of the mind which need to be known if we are to understand the laws under which mind operates. The first of these characteristics is that mind cannot distinguish between what is fact and what is imagined to be fact. Indeed, mind goes further than this; it is only the imagined truth which has validity for the mind.

Suppose, for instance, that you hear a strange noise in the dead of night. You imagine it to be a prowler and this frightens you. Your mind automatically gears up your body in response to that fear. Your pulse rate quickens, your breathing becomes shallow, your hands get clammy and your throat dry. When the true source of the noise turns out to be the family dog, inexplicably shut away in the hall closet, you may feel a bit sheepish (and terribly relieved!) but you can also see that mind is not being guided by objective fact at all but by what it imagines to be "objective fact."

Hypnotism offers a good example of the power of a belief. Hypnotism is a state of mind in which the subject temporarily suspends his own beliefs and substitutes, in their stead, the beliefs articulated by the hypnotist. In effect, the subject takes his own analyzer out of the way and lets the analyzer of the hypnotist call the shots. Under these circumstances, if the hypnotist says that an icicle is a red hot poker, the icicle will raise burn blisters wherever it touches the subject. If the hypnotist says that the pencil on the table is too heavy to lift, no matter how hard he tries, the subject will not be able to lift the pencil. If the hypnotist says that the subject has just eaten a hearty meal, then the subject's blood chemistry will actually reflect that fact, not the "truth" of the empty stomach. (Think about that one the next time you consider how best to diet!) Beliefs supplied by a hypnotist or by ourselves effect the outcome in exactly the same way. They function as actualizers. They fulfill themselves. They cannot be disobeyed by the believer unless he lacks conviction in their truth.

*   *   *

There are two other aspects of mind which must be appreciated if its laws are to be understood. It functions in a spaceless mode and a timeless mode. These circumstances profoundly alter the laws which govern mind's use of psychic energy from what you might expect based on the laws which govern the physical world. If you wish to learn how to use mind consciously, you must understand how spacelessness and timelessness affect the creating process.

We are very aware of our separateness. Indeed we all pay homage to this superficial illusion. You are you and I am I and we care deeply about these distinctions. What we commonly fail to appreciate, however, is our underlying and unseen indivisibility with All That Is and our intimate inter-relationship with all other outpictured I-ams which also arise from the same spaceless source, the endosphere. Mind recognizes no boundaries. Unless we understand this spaceless connection between ourselves and all else we will not be able to appreciate how events materialize which involve others.

Spacelessness explains, for instance, why thought transference or mind reading can work. We share the endosphere with all minds. Indeed, the truly remarkable talent is that we are able to distinguish at all those thoughts which belong to our individualized selves. Alas, for some this ability is sufficiently eclipsed so that they do indeed function primarily upon the thought patterns of others—a persuasive parent (dead or alive), a dominating spouse, or a guru perhaps. While such arrangements are usually long term, we can also experience a sort of short term static—a depression possibly. Such a mood may not be truly our own but belong more properly to someone closely tied to us—perhaps an unhappy child or an angry spouse. This phenomenon of spaceless interconnection is also why some social gatherings get off the ground and some are mordantly dull.

Our universal bonding in spacelessness explains how psychic healings are performed even when the healer is physically distant from his patient and why there is no time lag between the moment a mental message is sent and when it is received. Spacelessness also provides the basis for our ability to build collective events like wars as well as smaller events like auto accidents and chance meetings. The fact of spacelessness is why Jesus could, with integrity, invite his followers to be with him. Under the conditions of spaceless-timelessness, such an association can, in fact, take place from any historical vantage point.

Mob action is another phenomenon accounted for by the indivisibility of underlying mind as all minds take on the coloration of one mind for the moment. Spacelessness enables an orchestra to play as a unit or dancers to tango. In short, the union of all minds in one spaceless mind is why we can reach any sort of agreement. Without spacelessness we would be utterly bereft of all communication with each other.

I am always amused by the detailed accounts which describe a scientific exploration into a pyschic phenomenon like thought transference. A scientist may go so far as to take a subject down in a submarine, put him in a lead-shielded box or glass bell. The scientist is now confident that the subject can no longer send or receive messages from a land based co-conspirator. The scientist goes through all this fol-de-rol because he will not acknowledge an unseen world. Even the ease with which messages are sent and received under these conditions does not cause him to question his premise that there is only one universe—the physical universe.

Because mind is spaceless, our link to our environment is far more profound than even ecologists imagine. The truth is that we are *one mind* with it. Was it Edgar Cayce who suggested that the best foods for us were those that were grown close at hand? This is because each bio-region is the cooperative construction of all that inhabit it. Bio-regions are like extended bodies tuned to sympathetic agreement with other abiding forms of consciousness within the region. Theorists of animal evolution must understand this complex interconnection between I-ams before they can correctly identify the causes of mutation, dearth, plenty, etc. It is not the survival of the fittest which supports (or kills off) life; it is survival within a network of the most intimate and complex cooperation. We would not dream of thinking that the success of an orchestra depended upon the determination of its musicians to overcome each other in their attempts to be heard. Why then should we assume that nature demands such a cacophonous struggle? Belief in Darwinism is symptomatic of a race which fears it can survive only by getting rid of the competition. Such a race does not understand its own deeper need for cooperation as a life-support system.

*   *   *

The characteristics of timelessness make explanations a bit more complicated, particularly since it concerns cause and effect. In the timeless endosphere, cause and effect are one and indistinguishable. When they are transposed into spacetime, however, *effect becomes cause.* Let me explain. Imagine that you get the idea that it would be fun to give a party. Even while you think of it, you envision an end result. As a matter of fact, the end result (or effect) is what prompts the idea of a party in the first place. You think in terms of *effect*. The imagined result is mother to the inspiration. It is only when you act out your idea in physical reality that you must start at the "beginning" with a guest list and work your way through to the end when you finally hang up the dishtowel. Throughout all your efforts, however, you are pushed/guided, like a carefully monitored missile, by the end result—*the effect*—you have in mind. The imagined future is cause to the present.

Events are imagined end results which are sufficiently energized to activate a beginning. Events in the future are imagined in the now.

Any thought can start the creative process of materializing that thought's chosen end result but most thoughts die a-borning. On the other hand, thought-seeds which are adequately encouraged by the mind will germinate whether we like it or not. Thoughts summon pyschic energy. Once that energy is evoked *it must be used up in a manner which describes the originating thought.* Psychic energy has no other choice; it is the law under which psychic energy operates.

This is why our political posture of preparing for war in the name of peace is so insane. A war thought-seed cannot produce a peace flower. Those who advocate war, those who fear war, those who oppose war are all helping to nourish war by "making a big production" out of war. They energize, or activate, a thought-seed called war, for we can neither advocate, fear, or oppose an idea which is not real *to us*. The way to create peace is to embrace peace with an even greater fervor than we presently direct towards opposing and/or fearing war. In our minds we must make peace even more real than war. Then peace will have to follow.

The personal implications of the law which forces the future to the imagined end result are profound. When I effect a healing, I imagine (to the mind imagination is real) the desired end result in the "now" so vividly that—other circumstances being equal—

the "future" I imagine *must* come to pass. This forces the old symptoms to dissolve and give way to the end result I have chosen in my mind. *Imagination, made real by conviction, must manifest because it has already been made real at the causal level.*

*   *   *

Something should be said about the language of thought. Thought expresses itself far more accurately than words can ever do. In a very real way, everything our senses perceive is the out-pictured physical symbol of an interior thought. Therefore all physical things are but the symbols for those thoughts. While drug manufacturers can and do plant successful thought-seeds in our minds that it is the time of year to come down with a cold, colds can also grow out of thought-seeds we have planted about personal matters.

The effects of a bad cold mimic or "symbolize" the effect of a bad crying jag. If something happens which makes us feel like crying *and we do not cry,* then the body may be asked to express that crying for us by watery eyes, a sore throat, etc. Tears are no less a symbolic out-picturing of an interior thought than, let's say, a runny nose or a sore throat, but we tend to think of tears as the direct and hence "real" way to express grief. Thought makes no such distinction. If we do not let it express itself in one way, it will—indeed must—express it in another. We usually call that "other way" symbolic.

Thoughts are not, of course, limited to out-picturing themselves only in the body. There are no such boundaries for thought. They create external circumstances with the same ease that they create bodily conditions. Psychic energy, once evoked by the definition of a thought, reproduces whatever symbolic effect is easiest. If you believe, for instance, that you don't get sick—a condition which will also fulfill itself—then if you experience unpleasant feelings which you do not express "directly" in tears, instead of getting sick, you may have an auto accident or be rebuffed romantically or lose your job.

Psychic energy is interested only in discharging itself in the exact form and in the exact amount summoned. Specifically, this means that if you only feel a bit disgruntled with life, you may do nothing more than cut your finger. If you feel heavily burdened, the resultant psychic energy will produce an event of greater consequences. For this reason it is best to keep careful track of negative thoughts and not let them build up. Unfortunately, we are masters at self-deception and may not recognize that we are entertaining such thoughts. Moreover most of us like to consider ourselves brave in the face of adversity so that when we feel we have been hit below the belt, instead of dealing with this negative thought, we put on a smile as if nothing had happened. Yet these are exactly the kind of occasions which manifest "secretly" ("symbolically") as poor health, accidents, and the like.

Thoughts themselves are plastic; they are organic in nature. What started out in your mind as a small and intimate dinner party may grow to a big cocktail party. The refreshments for the cocktail party may change from wine and some snack crackers to a veritable smorgasbord of delectables. Nor does the idea with which you start necessarily guarantee your consciously anticipated end result. The thought of a group of happy people enjoying your hospitality may not have sufficient strength because of other intervening thoughts. You may end up with a flop of dismal proportions because you are also thinking, "I hate giving parties. I'm just not good at it," or "I just know Jim is going to get drunk and ruin it for everybody," etc.

The actual party may differ beyond recognizable form from the originally imagined party because the future is as plastic as it is compelling. Thoughts force an exploration of possibility as well as demand an end result. Thoughts and the psychic energy they command are blueprints for tomorrow as we think of linear time.

Yet truly, and contrary to the look of the physical world, in the greater reality of our timeless being, yesterday and tomorrow both rest in the eternal present where cause and effect are one.

*   *   *

All events are created in the identical way even if we are not consciously aware of what is happening. Therefore let's look at how the mind works a simple but miraculous event like fetching a book from the other side of the room. The thought *I will get the book* includes the completed effect you imagine in your mind and this effect becomes cause of all the action which ensues.

You see the book on the far table. Your mind assembles all the relevant information and formulates a plan of action. It begins to feed the body the necessary step-by-step (!) instructions. Your leg muscles—in fact, all your muscles—are apprised of the coming event and instructed on how to behave. Your heart increases the supply of blood to the activated muscles. The blood stream carries off waste products from this exertion. Your intestines may stop digestion to allow the body's resources to be used elsewhere. Your eyes are commanded to see the path in front of you so that your mind can properly evaluate the data and guide the body accordingly. Your ears measure your body's balance so that your mind can adjust its orders to the body. Every cell in your entire body is aware of what is happening and contributes to the end result your mind envisions.

"There is a chair. Walk around it," your mind orders. "Don't step on the crayon. Increase your stride to miss it." "A bit more blood, please." "Swing out your right elbow just a tad so your body won't fall." So good is the mind at engineering this feat that you don't have to "think" about it. You simply give the problem to your mind and it fulfills your wishes. Indeed, if you did think about it consciously, you could never get the task done. Try giving your leg a conscious instruction to walk. Do you flex the knee first or do you start with the pelvis? At what point does the ankle flex? But mind, compelled to make real the imagined future, conforms all action to this end result and "magically" manages the present to see that the future end result comes about. More than that, it *must* and will fulfill your expectations unless you stop it by a countering thought.

A friend called the other day to ask if I could help locate a folder of important papers. She hardly knew where to begin because she had been visiting all over the western United States with that folder and calls to various hostesses had left her without a clue. I told her I was no good at finding lost articles psychically but for what it was worth, I did feel the folder was close to her and in an upright position. I cautioned her not to take this information very seriously. I then told her how *she* could find it. She must stop seeing it as lost and start imagining very strongly that it was found. In the terms we have been using, she was to mentally produce the completed and desired end result in order to manifest that end result by forcing all necessary and intervening events to take place. If she continued to think of it as lost, she would of course continue to produce *that* result.

I bolstered her confidence by giving some examples from my own experience and told her that above all she was not to worry because worry was a mental statement that the folder wouldn't be found and would only increase the likelihood that this end result would prevail. She was to *know* that either her natural path would intersect with the location of the folder or that this would happen to one of her hostesses.

Two days later she called me in elation. She had been "inspired" (!), she said, to make a cake and for this particular cake she needed to get some nuts from her freezer. It was there she found the folder—standing upright!—a very pleasant validation for me. Don't ask me why she put the folder there. She doesn't know herself.

Exactly how the mental "event" of walking across the room to get the book manifests physically seems entirely logical because you are aware of both the motivating idea and you think you understand the series of motions leading to the end result. Everything is logical because you have all the information. It's what you expect. The sequence of events leading to the "miracle" of finding the folder seem unrelated to the programmed end result. It seems to you that my friend was thinking about making a cake and not finding the folder. Yet, the necessity of thinking about making a particular cake in order to find the folder might be compared to "thinking about" locomotion in order to get to the other side of the room. Both are necessary logistical problems which the mind must solve if it is commanded by the desired end result. The connection between baking a cake and finding a folder does not seem logical *unless* you know where the folder is. This is called a "miracle" only because this information is missing.

If we direct our minds consciously to see that we fetch the book and then watch the intervening events take place, already knowing what their purpose is, we call that normal. If we know we want the book but remain unaware of walking across the room and "wake up" with the book in our hands, we call that a miracle. If we are unaware that we even wanted the book but suddenly find that we are in possession of it, we call it an accident.

Now, using our knowledge that mind is not bound by space and the separation this space creates, and our knowledge that an imagined end result forces all intervening events, let's consider what I call a "collective event" where others besides ourselves are involved in the outcome.

I had long been aware of the mind's ability to awaken us at any hour we decided upon, obviating any need for an alarm clock. I wanted to move to a more complicated experiment. I had a meeting in San Francisco the next day, scheduled for 8:30 a.m. I determined that I wanted to be at that meeting exactly 15 minutes before it began. That didn't mean 8:15 because meetings never start on time and so I didn't know exactly when I should be arriving to accomplish my goal. I then told myself that I wanted to awaken at the appropriate time to accomplish this. I omitted the usual computations of so much time to eat and dress, so much time for travel, etc. Consciously, I had no idea what the right time to wake up might be.

When I did awaken, it was still dark and it seemed to my reasonable self that it was far too early to get up. After all, anxiety about when I should awaken might have caused me to jump the gun. Still, I went about a myriad of small tasks, more slowly perhaps than might be usual because it seemed so early. At 7:45 I was on the Bay Bridge and more or less in sight of the hotel where the meeting was to take place. I began to fear I might have an auto accident, for what else could absorb all this extra time? I easily found a parking place—strange with 400 people expected at the meeting—but it was not until I reached the hotel lobby that all this so-called extra time began to find its purpose. I was in the wrong hotel! My conscious mind had thought this the right hotel but my unconscious mind knew better and knew too that I would inevitably have to make this mistake before I reached my right destination. It programmed things accordingly.

With the off-again-on-again help of a busy hotel manager, it was some time before we discovered where the meeting was really taking place and even more time to give me elaborate directions. Incidentally, part of the charm of consciously programming the end result is that everyone else is involved in assisting you to achieve your ends. (And if you unconsciously program your end results negatively, they will help you do this, too! This means they will mug you or hit you with their automobile, etc.)

Out in my car once more, I somewhat nervously followed my directions, again found a parking place, but this time with more difficulty, and finally arrived at the meeting at exactly 8:27. The meeting, of course, started at 8:42, exactly 15 minutes after I arrived, just as I had planned in my "imagined end result."

"Imagining the end result" is precisely what aborigine tribes do in what they call Dream Time.[1] They "see" their prey, perhaps several mountains away, and then travel unerringly on a path which intersects with the path of the animal. They find water in the desert in the same way and can retrace, turn for turn, complicated pathways through forest, underbrush or desert sands another person has taken even some years earlier. Yet we are awed by the homing and migratory abilities of so many animals—salmon, whales, and pigeons, for instance. They seem remarkable to us simply because we do not use our own similar and innate capacities to effect these "miracles."

*　*　*

I think it brings the meaning of life into focus to see ourselves as creating creations. A belief that life has been imposed upon us either by accident (the scientific view) or by a God who set things out on a living room rug for his entertainment, forbids an understanding of the cosmos and our connection with its most fundamental purpose—the act of creating. Our lives are not created for us, but by us. The source of our lives is not beyond us but within us.

Although originally we are, I believe, the thought forms of other more powerful forms of consciousness, once created, we, much like our children, are free to go our individual ways, weaving in and out of history and in and out of physical reality as we experiment with the creative ability of the mind. Even so, in the truer reality of One, we maintain an intimate connection with our creating "over-soul" and All That Is.

I see us as an indivisible part of something which goes mad with the joy of creating, like the salt mill in the children's story which

[1]Joseph Chilton Pearce. op. cit.

couldn't stop make salt. In this regard only we have no choice. We must keep creating. We cannot sit on the sidelines. Death certainly does not stop the process. It merely takes us out of one reality and puts us in another. If we don't like this game, it's a pretty good bet we won't like the next one much better. It seems to me that under such circumstances, it's best to say, "Well, if that's the way it is and if I have this talent for creating whatever I wish, then I'd better get in there and start creating things I like and have a little fun."

I do not know where the dividing line is between what humans can create and what may be created by "super-thinkers." For instance, how much does an unswerving belief that the sun will rise tomorrow have to do with this happening? Are the movements of the solar system under our subconscious control, beyond our control or do we share in some proportion in that control? If so, who is included in that partnership?

We manufacture realities in our dream experiences which seem as real to us while we dream as the "real" world seems when we are awake. Does this mean that we are prepared to make real whatever reality we are in? If so, are the swirling planets only a collective mental fantasy made real because we have been "hypnotized" by mass belief? Many, many authors—Leo Tolstoy, for one—have believed that true reality was dream reality and that physical reality was more accurately described as a shadow reality. If this is true, then we have of course invented the whole ball of wax for our own amusement and edification. This is more or less my persuasion.

On a specific level, I *do* know we create diseases to satisfy our perceived need for illness—a need kept in place because we believe so thoroughly in disease. A scientist who believes he can rid us of disease by finding new drugs is working on a treadmill. As soon as he conquers tuberculosis or leprosy we will produce Legionnaire's Disease or Acquired Immune Deficiency Syndrome

(AIDS). I know too that we create our weather. (I think of weather as the barometric reading of the collective emotional energy level.) I know we enormously influence the animal and plant life around us because we participate so intimately in our bio-regions.

I have no wish to attribute to ourselves what rightfully belongs only within the power of greater capacities, but I find no line of demarcation in the hierarchy of possibility in which we partici-pate. Until we know much more, the suggestion that we are om-nipotent within our own realm serves, I think, as a better model of how the cosmos functions than any we have been given so far. Under these circumstances, I think it only fair to ask—which one of you guys thought up the hyena?

8.

Emotion

I T IS BEST to imagine that a clouded screen of beliefs stands between ourselves and the outside world because we do not see
outer reality factually. We see inner reality which we *describe* as
outer reality. Behind this shield we are in moment to moment
reaction to what this arrangement causes us to experience. Thus
not only is the source and cause of life emotional but the experience of life is emotional. Life *is* emotion—expressed.

If a seed did not have an *emotional* preference for fulfilling itself,
it could not grow. I grant you that seeds do not experience the ex-
citable range of emotions that humans do, but plenty of experi-
ments make it abundantly clear that plants are very *emotionally*
aware of what is going on around them. They react most violently
to being harmed themselves or to harm being done to other living
organisms around them. In both cases they go into electromagnetic spasms. Nor, incidentally, do they distinguish between the
thought and the deed of the experimenter. For a plant—naturally
tuned to cosmic law—thinking harm and doing harm are one and
the same.

From a more pragmatic and human point of view, the emotions
are energy and they measure directly the amount of energy summoned in the likeness of a particular belief. Because the management of life is the management of energy we need to know a bit

more about the part emotions play in the expression of life. For this we need to think of the emotions as charged with the control of a valve which regulates creating energy. Open up the valve with a passion and we have a great amount of energy which must be used up in a display of itself—a temper tantrum, a love scene, a crime of violence, etc. Close down the valve with indifference and survival itself becomes problematical, for the proper amount of energy is not coming through to sustain life adequately.

We deal with emotions in one of two ways: we act them out or we suppress them. If we act them out, the energy is soon expended as we "get rid of" those feelings. Since successful living depends in large part on finishing what is past so that we can be in the present, expending this energy immediately can be very positive no matter what the emotion. (I *would* suggest, however, that you direct violence towards a brick wall instead of your wife or child! Moreover, they are not your problem, your belief system is.)

Far too often, however, when we experience a negative emotion—and thereby open the energy valve—we forbid its expression. Or so we hope. The zinger in our attempt to suppress an emotion is that once an emotion has evoked energy, it is too late to put a damper on that energy. THERE IS NO SUCH THING AS AN UNEXPRESSED EMOTION!!! It is a genie out of the bottle and if you will not let it escape outwardly, it is you who will be its recipient, its victim. While there are advantages in not laying waste the landscape around you with your wrath, the indirect consequences can be enormous and you should at least be aware of the choices you make. I have just finished seeing someone who has cancer because she denied her unacceptable emotions and those emotions had no choice then but to express themselves towards herself.

From cut fingers to auto accidents, from life-threatening diseases to muggings, we beat ourselves to a pulp with negative emotions we dare not express directly. What's more incredible, we believe we are handling things so well when we do this. I repeat: emotions are energy. The sole purpose of energy is to create. If you do not create a "scene" and expend that energy, that energy will create the scene for you.

Additionally, withholding an emotional response increases its energy proportionally to the effort involved. The energy accompanying the original feeling must be countered with an equal amount of energy in order to deny it. It is force against force and it doubles the original capacity of that emotion.

We will have a great deal more to say about trouble-making negative emotions because they are an important diagnostic tool for discovering faulty beliefs. Negative emotions are symptoms of a mental "dis-ease" created by a belief system which is out of whack with the principles of the Creating Cosmos. The cosmos is *not* built on a dichotomy. It is human misconceptions which build dichotomies. Beliefs are either in sync with the cosmos or they are in opposition to its intent. If a belief is based on a cosmic falsehood, life will be unpleasant. I recommend Chapter 10 in *The Creating Cosmos* for an expanded explanation. For our purposes here, it is enough to remember that life management is energy management. Emotional energy management.

9.

The Psychic Energy Field

EVERY PHYSICAL FORM is supported, defined, and maintained by a subliminal thought form. That includes everything from planets to people. This form is called the astral form or astral body. The astral body is not physical nor is it subject to physical laws, which is why amputees can often feel the presence of their missing limbs. On the astral or mind level these limbs are still present because this is the level which acknowledges feeling.

All astral forms dwell within their own astral auras. These auras define a particular form's space. Auras should be thought of as psychic energy fields but they are not to be confused with the electro-magnetic auras picked up in Kirlian photography. The Kirlian "auras" are physical. Astral auras are made of finer matter—probably too fine to be detected by present-day scientific equipment. As the space of the solar system is to the sun, so an aura is to a human.

Auras should be thought of as our personal space—our home. Like homes, they not only offer protection, but they identify the owner. In addition they are both the storage closets for our unresolved emotional problems and the kitchen for our incipient thought "seeds," which are not sufficiently mature to reproduce themselves. (Psychics who read the future are either seeing or "feeling" these forms when they make their predictions.)

The aura is the final staging area in the inner creating process before endospheric events manifest physically. Energy here is neither totally mental or totally physical. Think of it as early physical. It is possible to weed out our gardens at this point by meditating on the aura. We will return shortly to the subject.

*   *   *

Persuaded by scientists, we have obligingly educated ourselves to believe that we cannot see what is scientifically impermissible. We therefore choose not to see auras. It is our way of attesting to our personal sanity to see in Rome only what the Romans say we can see. Nevertheless, each of us *is* seeing and being seen on this level whether or not we wish to acknowledge it consciously. For instance, "I don't know why, but there is something I just don't like about that man," or "Whenever I'm around her I always feel better." Both are statements which indicate that we are picking up information on this astral or mental level. Auras are open books and therefore we can keep no real secrets from each other. For this reason the aura is a very important communicating medium.

Auras also behave like protective shells. If the aura or our housing is not strong and vibrant, the body will be adversely affected. An aura can be well-delineated or it can be ragged. It can be vital or enervated. It can be airy or dense, vibrantly colorful or pale and muddied. It can be clear or swathed in grey or even black veils. It can even have sections which are damaged or missing altogether.

Within the aura are layers of color, each layer corresponding to a chakrah (shock-ra) or energy center of the astral body. (These very important energy centers will be discussed at length in Chapter 16.) Depending upon mental and physical circumstances, these bands of color can be thick or thin, they can be highly structured or without perceptible definition. Although I have never read a person labelled insane, a psychic trained in these matters could easily distinguish between such a person and someone who was only psychologically stressed because the aura reveals this kind of information. It is as easy for a psychic to see "psychic structural damage" as it is for any building inspector to find structural fault within a building.

The aura is simultaneously an intimate reflection of the mind and how it is functioning and a strong influence on the mind. It is the mind's environment. It is the bed the mind creates to lie in. Therefore a psychic who sees auras could, with equal accuracy, say, "There is a veil across your aura and this veil is creating confusion," or "You are confused and this is causing a grey veil to appear in your aura." On this level cause and effect are one.

In order to make permanent changes in the "atmosphere" (or aura) in which we dwell, beliefs will have to be changed and past experiences de-energized. On the other hand such changes can be greatly facilitated by cleaning up the aura itself. (Again, think of your home and the positive effect its attractive orderliness has on your sense of well-being.) Therefore even if you can't see an aura, knowing of its presence and something of its importance gives reason for meditating upon its health. (Meditation is but one form of energy manipulation.) Cleaning up an aura by stipulating that it be vibrant and sparkly will not make your problems go away, but it will certainly give you a temporary sense of well-being. Problem solving becomes much easier if you feel strong and confident. A clean aura can permit this.

To help familiarize you with a home you may not even know you have, we will explore auras in some detail. Even if you can't see them, knowing about them can be of great advantage in problem solving.

*   *   *

Under normal conditions the aura extends out from the body perhaps two or three feet in all directions although these boundaries are very flexible. Great entertainers instinctively extend their auras to include the entire theater, thereby putting their audiences "under the spell." All of us can do this consciously if we wish by stipulating that it be so. I once watched the symphony conductor Seiji Ozawa "capture" his orchestra and the first several rows of the audience within his aura. I was sitting in those rows and it was a magnificent evening. It felt as if I were literally *in* the music. I suspect that all good conductors do this instinctively so that orchestras can function as a unit under one energy system.

Mob action is another illustration of the extended aura phenomenon. Members of a mob (or an orchestra?) act in concert because they are temporarily surrendering their individual autonomies to create a unifed energy field or aura. Auras, as you might expect from this, can blend together or antagonize one another. Blended auras produce much better love-making! Confrontation creates auras which are incompatible in terms of energy. The energy becomes polarized.

Auras can also contract. Many people draw in their auras in the presence of others. These people are "shrinking violets" or those who "hide their light under a bushel basket." (Do you see how knowing our language reveals us to be?) If you are shy or easily intimidated by others, practice relaxing in the comfort of a strong and protective aura. You should not be pulling in your aura. Your aura is your rightful space. Claim it! If you don't, other people will have no choice but to move into the vacuum you create and you will then wonder why you feel so uncomfortable in the presence of others.

The aura provides physical as well as psychological protection. If you are not letting the aura do its job of protection because you are not claiming your rightful space, you *may* be creating fat to provide the same protective service. Skin problems can also result from an aura which is too thin to provide adequate protection. Think of the aura as a sun screen which protects the body from "harmful radiation."

Most people gather in their auras around their upper bodies like an old army blanket because they feel insecure. They leave their legs and feet unprotected. These people invariably have cold feet—physically and tempermentally. (Notice again how beautifully our language conveys exactly what is happening. We see and see not that we see.)

A weak aura may also lead to ulcers and other stress diseases because the body feels too threatened in its unprotected state. All else being equal, a strong aura is all that is needed to thwart the intent of muggers, rapists, and other random sadists. Such sadists are looking for victims or people with weak auras and will intuitively avoid those with strong auras. They, like the rest of us, are attracted or repelled by the subliminal look of the aura. They just happen to be attracted to weakness. Unfortunately, we have been culturally indoctrinated to believe that being old is synonymous with being useless in a society which idolizes youth. Accordingly, older people act out this cultural belief and thereby create "useless" auras. Such conduct, created by these beliefs, make the elderly prime targets for bullies.

Some people have auras so cluttered with charged memory pictures that their auras form almost impenetrable walls. Others can't reach these people, neither can they themselves reach out. They live in their own little worlds with the pain of the past so alive that there is little possibility of dealing with the present. These Stuck Pictures (see Chapter 11) have, as their base, unfaced emotional dread. Unfaced, these emotions present themselves as current problems because they build up as black or grey veils (stagnant energy) throughout the aura. This cluttering not only drags down our present-day enjoyment of life but seriously hastens disease. You may think of a Stuck Picture as a thrombosis of the aura. In truth, there is no division between the energy of the aura and the energy of the body.

Ideally, we should all be free of these "sore spots" for they keep us operating in the past and significantly diminish our present energy level. People who are chronically tired are not likely to be suffering from an improper diet or exercise so much as they are from painful pictures. This would be true for all named diseases which express the symptom of lassitude. As a former sufferer from chronic fatigue myself, I have, over the years, tried almost every diet and regime recommended. It was only after I began to deal with Stuck Pictures that I was able to put aside decades of weariness. Now at the age of 60 I have more energy than I had when I was in college and I pay little attention to either diet or exercise. Nor have I seen a doctor in the last 15 years.

I think of two experiences which illustrate this kind of Stuck Picture as it appears in the aura and the mischief it causes. In a moment of candor, a Jewish friend of mine admitted having bigoted feelings towards Catholics. She really didn't trust them, she said. Her bigotry distressed her because she was otherwise a tolerant person and was particularly sensitive, as a Jew, to such bigotry. However, the more she attempted to explain the nuances of her feelings, the more brightly shone a Christian cross in her aura above her head. (This is where we carry particularly significant symbols.) I was very surprised because she took much pride in her Jewish heritage and had often declared that if it were indeed true that we lived more than once she would never be anything but a Jew.

I was curious, therefore, and could not resist looking (psychically) into this matter. I found three "past lives" which were of particular interest. In one of these lives she had been a French Huguenot (a Protestant) at the time of the vicious persecutions by the established Catholic majority. In at least two other lives she had also been persecuted for holding Christian beliefs in opposition to the paganism of Rome and the Judaic beliefs of the Middle East. Then, as now, she proudly identified with a martyred minority religion which had stood up for its beliefs at considerable costs. The specific religion she selected seemed not to be so important to her as the identity with a persecuted minority, for she had been the victim of Jew and Gentile alike.

In this life she was moving away from the need to be involved with active religious persecution. She chose, for instance, to be born in the United States rather than Nazi Germany. She had also married a Protestant—a member of the "persecuting" majority. Thus, the idea of martyrdom was very definitely losing some of its appeal. Still, to the extent that Christian Martyrdom remained active, she was using present day energy for "past" purposes. At the very least her attitude about Catholics—formed in the "past"—was getting in the way of a full range of friendships.

The second demonstration of a Stuck Picture within an aura happened during my training at the Berkeley Psychic Institute. Lew Bostwick, the founder of the Institute, was lecturing to us from the center of a large circle. I was having some difficulty grasping the gist of what he meant when he suddenly interrupted himself with the command to freeze. This caught me with my head cocked characteristically over to one side. "Okay," he continued, "Everyone look at Barbara. Do you see that picture over her shoulder which is forcing her head to bend in that way? It's a picture of a woman who is about to hit her." I burst into tears, knowing it was my mother even as he was explaining the picture. I also knew I was about to be hit because I had done something wrong and I didn't know what. Because that picture had become stuck, I had, for 50 years or so, associated getting muddled in my head with being hit. I "just naturally" cocked my head to the side (to avoid the blow) whenever I didn't understand what was being said to me. Not only can Stuck Pictures force physical behavior, they can interfere with the proper functioning of the body in their immediate area. Stuck Pictures clog the proper flow of energy— energy needed for the health of the body.

For those of you who enjoy meditation, focusing your attention on your invisible aura can bring about a noticeable improvement in how you feel. Picture the aura as clear, well-defined, brilliant in its coloration, and alive with good energy. Stipulate that it extend well around your entire body—including your feet—and that it be inviolate to all but positive experiences. In your imagination take the gunk you have cleaned from your aura and put it into a container. (If you merely pile this stuff outside your aura, it will form its own berm of negative energy and you will find yourself living in a fortress.) Now explode the container—in your imagination, of course! The reason for doing this is that you wish to neutralize negative energy with positive energy. It signifies YOU are in charge. Do this repeatedly until you feel smart and sassy and *powerful*. Victims collect depressing pictures. Winners can afford to let them go. *Playing at being a winner* will automatically change many of your beliefs about the benefits of being a loser. And that is the very basis of problem solving.

Think HAPPY. Think STRONG. Your aura will reflect this and give those around you real pleasure. Most importantly, it will give you real pleasure.

10.

Games Egos Play

T HERE IS ANOTHER creative process taking place within the endospheric reality which must now be accounted for. It has to do with the ego and its insistence on having its needs met. The ego uses—I could say abuses—the creative process to suit itself. Eastern religions attempt to circumnavigate the problems caused by the ego by 'doing away' with it. As the ego is necessary to keep the self integrated with physical reality, this expectation, to my mind, obviates physical experience. As we shall see, there are other, better solutions.

Because we must become (something else) in order to exist at all, the self must decide what to become. This demands self-awareness. And self-awareness demands that some part of the self become the observing self and look back upon itself in order to make evaluations and criticisms. The observing self (the ego) makes judgments and proposes an improved or anticipated self so that the proper direction can be provided towards specific goals. The disparity between the witnessed self and the idealized self creates the self-image.

Imagine now that the self-image forms a bridge between the witnessed self and the idealized self. Imagine also that the ego stands on this bridge. If the span is great, the bridging self-image will be weak and the ego will feel itself to be in danger because of the straddling act it is forced to perform. It will continually call for help. It will feel threatened by small incidents. It will continually be looking for some kind of reinforcement. On the other hand, if the span between the two parts of the self is not great, the ego will feel comfortable and well sustained. The self-image will be strong and positive. Life can be something more than an emotional roller-coaster.

Unfortunately, religious institutions have had their considerable impact on both fashioning the idealized self and depreciating the witnessed self. They have spread the span between the two, weakening the ego. Weak egos make good supplicants, but they make troubled and unhappy souls which in turn create social, economic, and political problems of unmeasurable proportions. If you aspire to *spiritual* health, you will have to look very closely at the religious indoctrination you have undergone—whether or not you currently attend church.

The purpose of the physical illusion we call the real world is to make our subjective experience graphic. These external experiences include the dreads and delights the self is encountering because of its ability to imagine—a capacity so enormous it cannot possibly be put into effect in a limited physical reality by one self. The solution to this is to duplicate the breadth of imaginative possibility by having each of us represent a facet of that imagination. We cannot, each of us, be the butcher, the baker, and the candlestick maker, but if you are the baker and I am the butcher we can live within the spectrum of possibility. Moreover, we can all interact physically with these representations to get a clearer view of our internal choices.

Other people, then, are stand-ins for the internal complexities of our subjective reality. They are the cast which provides the attenuated, diagrammed, mock-up of our inner drama. This is their purpose in our experience of physical reality and this is why other people are so important to us. This is also why we love and hate them. They represent aspects of ourselves which we cherish or deny.

The ego, sitting on the bridging self-image, is a direction finder. Its *true* purpose is to guide the self, by careful selection, on a path into and through physical reality which is right for the self. The ego, therefore, is externally oriented. Because we usually think with our egos, we believe, as the ego does, that the external drama is the real drama. To the ego, the pains and pleasures of life seem to be coming from beyond the self—inflicted or bestowed by others. It is, of course, possible that the witnessed self and the idealized self are so far apart that no adequate bridging apparatus can be formed. When this happens the ego is unable to function as the pathfinding link between the self and the physical world. Insanity is the result. Insanity is a critical "dis-ease" of the ego.

The *self-assigned* purpose of the ego is to make itself comfortable, which it can only manage if the span between the witnessed self and the observed self is small. It never seems to occur to the ego to reduce its expectations to something more realistic. I suppose the weaker it feels the more it believes that lofty expectations will solve its problems. Instead its entire effort seems dedicated to making the witnessed self *appear* ideal (perfect). It would, quite literally, rather send the self to certain death than suffer the anguish of *appearing* less than perfect. The weaker the ego the more it involves itself in this game, a game it plays in relation to other people.

There are two ways to deal with other people. These ways depend on two different points of view. One point of view arises out of what I call survival purpose. The other point of view arises from transcendent purpose. We play the game of me-OR-you or the game of me-AND-you. We go for winners and losers, or winners and winners. Survival purpose is the game of an ego who stands on a wobbly bridge between the ideal self and the witnessed self but it is also the game we have been enculturated to play. To the weak ego, life is a power game. If the weak ego isn't continually validated in its opinions and actions—if it isn't declared a winner—it automatically becomes a loser. As a loser, the weak ego feels debased, wronged, and impotent. The goal of the me-OR-you game is to keep on being a winner against everyone who may threaten to challenge that winning position. If it doesn't do this it involuntarily becomes a loser, by virtue of a belief in winners and losers. *All* of our negative emotions come from the feeling that we have lost this game of me-OR-you. If we didn't organize our lives around survival purposes we wouldn't have emotional problems. We must therefore return to the me-OR-you game and explore it in depth, but before we do, let's look at the alternative game of transcendent purpose.

Survival purpose is competitive. There must be winners and losers. Transcendent purpose is cooperative. Transcendent purpose is founded upon a me-AND-you point of view. There are no losers. There are only winners. It is a commitment of positive caring. It is perhaps most easily and naturally expressed through the love a parent expresses for a child. But that's so simple. Loving a baby, whose purposes pretty much coincide with parental purpose, presents none of the difficulties that loving an equal *as an equal* can evoke. This is where we start to get into trouble.

Gandhi described transcendent purpose (he called it satyagraha) as *the simultaneous posture of fierce autonomy and total compassion. Transcendent purpose considers the needs and integrity of others as equal in importance to the needs and integrity of the self.* It makes no distinction between me and thee. It transcends these artificial barriers and functions on a plane where common purpose has a higher value than personal purpose. Transcendent purpose acknowledges that one's own welfare is diminished by the suffering of any other person.

It can be assumed, for the purposes of illustration, that white people within the Civil Rights Movement were impelled by transcendent purpose. At least until they had to confront a bigot! The white liberal was then apt to descend to hating the redneck with the same fervor that the redneck felt in hating a black man. Such a liberal descended, then, to a me-OR-you mental set, no better than his enemies. He too meant to have winners and losers.

(I cannot resist asking you to compare the effectiveness of passive resistance to the conventional [survival] methods of achieving political objectives. How many years have the Irish been fighting? Or the Israelis? Or the Central Americans? Or the Atlantic Treaty Nations which have been fighting off and on since 1914? How many lives have been lost? How many resources expended? What goals have been achieved in these struggles? Compare these fruitless efforts with those of Gandhi and Martin Luther King, Jr., who quickly achieved what they wanted with little sacrifice.)

Martin Luther King, Jr. was a notable example of a man given to transcendent purpose but he was unable to keep the movement he inspired from descending to the level of survival purpose. Those close to him grew impatient. They wanted more action. They wanted winners and losers. King's inability to keep his movement in a condition of transcendent purpose was, I believe, why he chose death at the hands of an assassin. Death is always a personal choice. To have it otherwise would be a denial of the principle on which the universe is founded—freedom to express the self in any manner it chooses. The act of death is a facet of that expression. The manner of death will, if you look closely, be an accurate expression of the life. For some, death may be a social protest. For others it is merely a decision to go on to something else. Some choose a very physical and quick end by a violent "accident." They will choose to be shot or fall in a mountain accident. Others feel themselves to be a victim of advancing years and will choose long illnesses to illustrate this. The reasons for dying are as personal as the reasons for being born. Both decisions arise from the self who is writing the script.

Autonomy—fierce autonomy—or the full appreciation of personal worth is absolutely essential to the achievement of total compassion. Only when the ego is strong can the ego afford to be compassionate. Only when there is self-love can the fear of others be reduced sufficiently for that love to flow outwardly. Those who doubt themselves cannot afford to have another succeed because it is interpreted as a personal loss.

The pay-off for being in a state of transcendent purpose is enormous. For one thing you are not threatened by the fear of losing, for that is no longer possible. There are, therefore, none of the difficulties which anxiety creates. For another thing your ego is no longer in pain and you can therefore flow into a situation instead of separating yourself from it in order to manipulate it. You are totally at ease. This gives you a power base which is extraordinary. It's like cruising along in overdrive instead of having to push the old junker up the road.

It is quite possible to experience satisfaction in a state of survival where a view of life is centered upon the self and its personal triumphs. But it is not possible to be truly joyous under such conditions. True joy—I really want to say the state of being blissed out—is a by-product of transcendent purpose. It is being "in love" permanently for it fuels itself.

Survival purpose is based upon need and need must be constantly satisfied with new reassurances. Such hunger is never dissipated for long and the search must continue. Transcendent purpose can take many forms—caring about the environment, love of animals, or serving mankind. But those who will find the greatest opportunity for joy will be those whose purposes take them out of themselves and towards other people—who dare to love others as passionately as they dare to love themselves.

Transcendent purpose is not easy. It demands great amounts of self-love and self-confidence. It demands maturity. Nonetheless, I present it to you as a challenge lest you think there is nothing beyond the thrill of a me-OR-you challenge. The adventure in loving they neighbor as thyself is far more sophisticated and therefore far more interesting than mere survival purpose. Besides, when purpose functions as it is intended to function, there is such joy in the harmony it creates.

11.

Making Ourselves Winners

THE ME-OR-YOU GAME is a power struggle to see who is right and who is wrong, who is a winner and who is a loser. The intent is to be superior to those we would make losers. The weaker and more threatened the ego feels itself to be, the more the self becomes involved in the me-OR-you game. Yet the more narrowly the ego divides action into Right Action and Wrong Action, the more rules it is forced to obey itself.

The full enjoyment of life rests on a personal freedom to choose. If all possibilities have been divided into Right Action and Wrong Action we have immediately diminished possibility by 50%. We have also diminished freedom by 100% because we no longer have *any* choice. We have only rules which must be obeyed. People who play the right/wrong game—and that's most of us, most of the time—have lost their freedom and the self-actualizing power which comes from being free.

In addition, when we play the right/wrong game, we center our finite energies on a battlefield where the trophy is, in any case, self-assigned. You may think you've scored big points by staying in a bad marriage when your father didn't, but does *he* know (or care) how great you are for this fine display of loyalty? Is he suffering or are you? Self-assigned trophies can be handed out as easily before the game as after it. So why go through all that folderol to make a point which escapes everyone's notice but your own?

War, of course, is the ultimate me-OR-you game—the ultimate right/wrong game—but the game is played daily at the most mundane level. Who should have called? Who should be showing more consideration? Who shouldn't drink so much at parties? Such assignments of Wrong Action give you some idea of how widespread the game is. It is, in fact, pandemic. It is breathed into almost every relationship. Even on this level it is destructive because it makes winners and losers. Winners become self-righteous and losers are denigrated. Think of it this way: every time you manage to score a point and make your mate or child or friend wrong, you have made yourself an associate of a loser. What kind of company do you keep, anyway?

There are two basic approaches to making ourselves right (winners). First, we can direct our energies towards making others wrong (as our observing self is doing to us). The assumption here is that if they are wrong—and we are willing to hold the opposite view—then we, by inference, *must* be right. You can rest assured that we will make them wrong (if that is our wish) even if we have to assume an untenable "right" position to do so. "I will too marry Johnny. Just because he's in prison is no reason not to be his wife!" In these games it doesn't seem to matter much what position we hold as long as it is opposite to the view held by the opponent. It is *he* we wish to make wrong, not a belief we care to validate. We can also make others wrong by blaming them for our misadventures. "It's your fault!" Secondly, we can make ourselves right either by getting others to agree that we are right or by an interior process I call lying. Usually we use these choices in combination but because each approach has its own consequences, we shall make these rather arbitrary divisions the better to understand what it is we do.

But a reminder! Although we play out our inner experiences with others as if those others were the problem, they are not. They are but the shadows of our inner turmoil. It is very important to remember this in all problem solving for the cause of *all* distress is within ourselves. But because we can only know what we are doing inside by looking outside, we will be discussing other people as if, in fact, we were dealing with them.

*   *   *

One way to make others wrong is to adopt a position opposite to theirs and stick by it. This can either be a virtue which we think is missing from their code of ethics or it can be in defense of our own delinquencies. We make them wrong (if only in our own minds!) by the sheer weight of our determination to *prove* them wrong. In order to defend a Wrong Action—one that *we* truly believe to be wrong—we must be willing to absorb the punishment we think Wrong Action deserves. Then, having paid the penalty, we are free to defend our position as Right Action. Such people are still playing the right/wrong game but they are playing it backwards.

Alcoholics, anorexics, criminals, compulsive gamblers top the list of examples of this kind of self-destructive behavior but the list also includes those with any defeatist habits which can't be broken—falling in love with the wrong woman, spending beyond one's means, being unable to lose weight, for example. Even carrying the torch for some long departed lover is a symptom of this self-destructive behavior.

Self-destructive types know they are wrong but as long as the guilt of this is allayed by self-punishment they can make themselves right (maintain their pride) by championing Wrong Action. No matter how painful the punishment, it is still less painful than admitting the original error. If you are self-destructive, ask yourself if making a self-defeating wrong into a right is worth the pain it creates for yourself. Is that pain *really* less than the pain of accepting responsibility for the original Wrong Action you are trying to make into a Right Action? Can you stand to lose a round in the right/wrong game or do you prefer to hang in there and make your entire life miserable in order to pretend that you are right? The choice is yours. No one but you is making you a victim of the game you play.

*   *   *

Another way of making others wrong (and ourselves right) is to blame them for our misfortunes. Characteristically, we blame our parents for the insufficiencies of our childhood. We blame society for its selfishness. We blame mates for our marital problems. We blame our children for their lack of gratitude. We blame the Japanese or the Arabs for our economic difficulties, the Russians for our international problems, and God for His indifference. We blame our misfortunes on germs, the other political party, the other driver, the greedy rich, the indolent poor, the unions or management, the ecologists or the developers. One woman even blamed the publisher of a cookbook. She sued him because the recipe she tried out on her husband's boss failed and she reasoned that this was why her husband didn't get his promotion. (I refrain from comment!)

Our popular love songs are filled with blame for the course of true love. "You broke my heart," "You're mean to me," "You made me love you," etc. Organizational hierarchies are arranged as much to assign blame as to effect command. Even our laws support our position of innocence in the most personal of matters. Bartenders are blamed for their customers' drunkenness, manufacturers are blamed for the careless storage of their products, so that we must all deal with those awful caps. Employers are blamed for their employees' self-abuse (stress, alcoholism, etc.). Blaming others has become a way of life which no one questions any longer. It sometimes seems to me that the whole world stands at attention, eyes, big with innocence, fingers pointing at the next guy, and saying, "Not me! HIM!!"

We pay a high price for the privilege of blaming someone or something else for our difficulties. The underlying statement we make is that germs, mates, bosses, other drivers, etc., have a greater power and can use that power more effectively than we. Every time we blame something external to ourselves, we give away some of our own power to control our destinies. Blame God and we become his toys. Blame the weather or germs and we become the prey of our very environment. (Germs, incidentally, are just as numerous around healthy people as they are around the sickly.) Blame other nations and we concede that we are a second-rate power. Blame the government and we announce that we are its subjects. Blame our families and friends and we cast ourselves in the role of victim to their designs.

Small wonder so many of us live in fear. We have given all our power away to others and when all these others are added together their numbers become oppressive. We are selling our birthright, our power, for a little temporary innocence. The truth is that each of us creates his own reality from the thoughts he wishes to out-picture. Recognizing this automatically makes each of us a power source. We can use that power to create whatever we wish. We do not need to be afraid, for others do not, indeed cannot, deprive us of advantage. We deprive ourselves of advantage by feeling, and hence expressing, powerlessness. To the degree that we blame others, we express our perceived inadequacy. Actually, we are *very adequately* expressing ourselves when others "get their way." We are expressing our wish to play the victim.

The choice is ours. We can take responsibility for what befalls us and be comforted by the awareness of our own power to create whatever we wish (even if it's bad!) or we can avoid responsibility, experience our inadequacy to deal with life, and continue our futile efforts to fight off fear and guilt.

*   *   *

There is a personal variation of the throw-the-blame-to-someone-else ploy. We can demonstrate the Wrong Action of others by *becoming* their victims. We make of ourselves the palpable reminder of their abusive behavior. It's a lovely game. We get to throw guilt pictures! I call such people practicing victims. Anyone who feels sorry for him or herself is, to some degree, a practicing victim. Aside from being victors in the right/wrong game, the only reward in this strategy is a justification for self-pity. The name of this game really should be called How-To-Win-By-Losing.

While the role of the practicing victim is by no means limited to women, it is a role which has become incorporated into the ethos of what it means to be female. Women are starting to change this through the feminist movement, but as usual in the right/wrong game, women blame men for their circumstances—the usual view of the practicing victim. Until women find cause for their victimization within themselves, they beg the question of a true solution.

Because feminism plays such an important role in contemporary society, it may serve a positive purpose if we take a small detour and look into what I believe to be some of the mistakes which initially got the ball rolling the wrong way. Characteristically, men are expected to thrust forward against circumstances and women are expected to wait upon deliverance. Thus women are expected to assume the ready-made posture of the victim. These sexist (and perverted) expectations arise, however, from very natural male/female principles. They are described by the Chinese as Creative and Receptive, and symbolized as Heaven and Earth. These two aspects of a whole are part of each of us. The female principle has nothing to do with submission. It has to do with pliancy, nurturing, generosity. (Think of the rich and supportive earth.)

Women, I believe, became the chattel of men for two immediately apparent reasons. First, they traded in their equality to *increase* their advantage over men and secondly, to assuage the guilt which this advantage aroused, they twisted the female principle of receptivity into submission.

It is a fact that a woman who is pregnant or nursing a baby cannot run from tigers and bears as fast as a man can. She and her baby need protection. The easiest way for a woman to guarantee this protection is to invent a marriage contract and thereby establish a cultural ethic which guarantees this protection. A woman would also wish to divide the labor of survival in such a way that *her* limitations, under the conditions of childbearing, were accommodated. To achieve all of these benefits to *her,* I do not doubt that women felt it psychologically expedient to put themselves under their protector's leadership as a sort of payment-for-services rendered.

But perhaps even more significantly, the mother/child relationship is without equal in its emotional intensity. Unless something disturbs the natural bonding process between mother and child, husbands/fathers are secondary in both the eyes of the mother and baby, at least in the early years. So what do you do if you've inveigled a man into marriage and then you transfer your emotional focus to your child who also loves you, not him, passionately? You dilute his potential for jealousy and your own feelings of guilt by indenturing yourself still further. The *quid pro quo* becomes, "I, the woman, will submit to you the man, if you will not notice the defection which is going on right under your nose."

Now that technology has greatly reduced the need for a protector, women want to change the rules of the traditional contract they originally set up. And they will. They have always gotten their way—then and now. Women get their way because of their role in the reproductive process. They are, undeniably, the prime sex. But now, with machines taking over so much of the "masculine" domain of active doing, we need more than ever to understand the female principle of caring and sensibility—qualities which cannot be machine-duplicated. What we do *not* need is the continuing disavowal of female characteristics in favor of masculine ones. It would have been nice for instance if we had permitted Geraldine Ferraro to be female instead of demanding that she demonstrate her ability to be one of the boys.

Practicing victims, be they male or female, may be the prototypic Jewish Mother, the chronic invalid, or the woman who stays with a wife beater. But the practicing victim is also anyone who wears that noble put-upon look or who takes pains to list his sacrifices or your sins of neglect. Wherever there is contrived "selflessness" there is also the practicing victim. ("Don't mind me. You just go ahead without me. What I want doesn't really matter anyway.") The practicing victim is playing the right/wrong game by representing the consequences of the opponent's wrong action. "You are wrong because you've hurt me. See how much I hurt!" At the root of a victim's attitude is his unwillingness to take responsibility for filling his own needs. He wants his irresponsibility to be right. Therefore if his needs don't get filled it's his opponent's fault. Lotsa luck!

The practicing victim manipulates through making his opponent feel guilty. (Guilt is the feeling that we are wrong.) If you are dealing with a practicing victim and his insinuations of guilt, take responsibility for your own acts and get yourself out of the right/wrong game *you* are playing. Your acts do not have to be considered as either right or wrong; they are simply actions that you have decided to take. If the in-fighting gets intense, give a warning: "I don't appreciate your trying to make me feel guilty."

If you are a practicing victim yourself, you can stop the abuse — real or imagined — whenever you wish by understanding that only you can tend your needs, for only you know what those needs are. Stop setting traps. "I really don't want to go to the movies but I won't tell you this. I'll go with you and be a sullen companion because you made me do it." It is neither fair nor possible to ask someone else to fill our needs for us (unless we are children — is that your game?) particularly when we lie about them. If you want something, see that you get it for yourself instead of making your opponent guess what your dishonest behavior implies. You have a right to what it is you want just like the rest of us. But you also have responsibilities.

There is a paradox in the victim's position which is well appreciated—at least unconsciously—by both parties. It is the victim who has the true power, not the master, because the victim can stop being a victim and end the master's reign whenever he chooses. And the master can do nothing about it. The abused wife can walk away. The humiliated can refuse to be humbled. The master's position rests on the cooperation and support of the victim. The victim creates the master, not the other way around. To end a master's reign, the victim need only step beyond the right/wrong game himself.

*   *   *

So far we have dealt with how we make ourselves right by making others wrong. We have other options. We can *make* ourselves right. The operative word here is *make*. *Being* right is not a problem! *Making* ourselves right requires some fancy mental gymnastics. In our effort to make ourselves right we have another recourse. We can seek validation from others by asking them to deny our fears and justify our hopes. "Make me feel that I am lovable by caring about me." "Make me feel sexually attractive by going to bed with me." "Make me feel that I am worthy by approving me."

As most of us play the power game of right and wrong, sexual relationships are also usually power games. This means that validation plays its significant role in sexual attraction. There is nothing more exciting than mutual validation with some good sex thrown into the bargain. And there is nothing more terrible than when our beloved runs off with another, taking away his validation and bestowing it elsewhere. This couldn't happen if we weren't counting on someone else to make us worthy.

Validation is important to all of us but when it becomes a necessary crutch for our sense of well-being, it also means that someone else has the power to withhold the same feeling of well-being. How many of us, for instance, are still trying to win parental approval because we equate their approval with our own worth? Reliance upon others to validate ourselves is like having our life savings in somebody else's name.

Far too many relationships are based on a mutual validation (or invalidation) arrangement. I call them needing relationships. To the degree that we need others, we are not free to love them. Love is a voluntary choice. Need—physical or emotional—weakens us to the point of dependency. Dependents may be terribly grateful but their despondency forces them to think primarily of themselves. Love is an out-going response, a response which a needing person cannot make. Needers cannot hold a hand in joy because they must grasp it as a life line.

The terrible pain of rejection—so much worse in its anticipation than in its fact—comes from our fear of losing the emotional support we need in order to feel worthwhile. Being rejected does not prohibit our ability to go on loving. Rather it denies us a source of validation which, while it lasted, seemed to prove that we were lovable. As we are lovable in direct proportion to our ability to love ourselves, being lovable is something we manage for ourselves. The rest of the world only mirrors back to us our own thoughts. Being "in love" is also self-generated. It is we who decide upon this response. It isn't something which is done to us. We are therefore free to be "in love" in any direction at any time.

* * *

We have one more scheme for making ourselves right. We can cover the picture of what we imagine to be a feared truth (a wrong) with another picture which we know to be a lie. What we do in this process is attempt to deny this terrible, feared truth—something we find horribly "wrong" about ourselves, something which arouses terrible guilt—by "erasing" it. Then we strive to live by the rules of this new self-image we wish were true. We become fanatical about being good, being right (and therefore guiltless) in this particular department. You would think we would at least play straight with ourselves but the fact is we lie in this way whenever it makes us feel better, whenever guilt becomes too disturbing. This is often.

We do all of this in the name of the right/wrong game. We mean to be right so that we don't have to experience guilt. We also mean to be right in order to save face, for pride is the prize of the right/wrong game. Lurking in our minds is the image of someone (usually a parent) who *would* be right if ever we were found out to be wrong.

The feared truth with which the "liar" copes can be anything which arouses intolerable guilt or the fear of being wrong. "I'm a rotten sonofabitch." "I'm so powerful I can inflict pain whenever I wish." "I'm a sexual pervert." The covering picture, and the behavior which these pictures compel, might be respectively, "I'm the nicest person anyone could know." "I'm too ineffectual to hurt anyone." "I hate sex." Together these pictures create what is called a Stuck Picture. At the base of this kind of Stuck Picture is the right/wrong game. Our feared truths are not feared, incidentally, because they are actually wrong. We *believe,* because of our belief systems, that they are wrong. Being wrong (in our minds) we are apt to embellish them to the point of caricature. For instance, "I feel sexual" becomes "I'm a sexual pervert."

There is another kind of Stuck Picture. It is created, not from a guilt picture, but from a wipe out picture—an incident which devastates a person's sense of effectiveness or power. This wipe out picture is covered with a success picture, frequently with an eye to making the perpetrator of the defeat wrong or avoiding any risk of repeating the incident. We look for a resurrection of pride and we accomplish this most often with a vow. A love affair which ends badly can be covered with "I'll never love anyone again!" An incident of mockery can be covered with "I'll show him I'm no sissy!" This complex, too, becomes stuck. Here the object is not the alleviation of guilt, but the restoration of a power base. In order to bring back feelings of effectiveness, we cover feelings of impotence with fantasies which offer comfort. We are rendered impotent in these situations because we believe in winners and losers. We do not understand that the very act of being alive signifies effectiveness.

This is how a Stuck Picture works. Beliefs (pictures) act like valves. They manage the flow of psychic energy. If the system is functioning properly, a particular belief will spring to the forefront as the immediate occasion demands. It will offer its guidance and subside. The valve which regulates psychic energy will close down. However, when we attempt to hold back a conscious recognition of a too-feared truth by blocking it with a counter suggestion, the valve is jammed in the open position because the emotional energy has yet to be fully experienced.

We must begin to think of the psychic energy system as being much like a plumbing system. Its smooth functioning depends on keeping it clean. This means dealing *honestly* with whatever comes up *as it comes up*. Something we believe to be a lie causes the system to gum up. Something we believe to be a truth dissolves once we experience it.

A Stuck Picture has two consequences. First, the covering (good) picture must be energized to the point of fanaticism for it is there to counter a highly charged emotional picture—a picture which must be denied at all costs. It forms a giant hairball in the plumbing system of life. (We shall return to this aspect of Stuck Pictures in Chapter 14.) Second, the feared truth, never having been dismantled, continues to reproduce itself emotionally and physically. We continue to feel sexually perverted in spite of celibacy and we continue to attract sexually provocative circumstances. *We continue to create our feared truths externally because they are still alive internally.*

Stuck Pictures can last a lifetime—perhaps many lifetimes. If you are driven to uphold a particular virtue you are dealing with a Stuck Picture. True virtue is a low-key affair. It's no big deal. It comes like a breath—naturally. If any memory—real or imagined—still brings up a charged emotional response you are dealing with a Stuck Picture. Somewhere your energy system has a valve that is jammed open because a picture didn't get properly recorded. You altered it so badly in an effort to feel better about yourself that you lied.

The originating circumstances which create a serious Stuck Picture almost always begin with our parents—at least in this particular lifetime. By the time we get around to solving them, however, we may have hundreds of similar pictures piled on top of one another. Whatever we currently think of our parents, it must be remembered that we loved and *needed* them intensely when we were children. Because of this need our battles with them were particularly intense. To search out a Stuck Picture, we may start in the present, but until we get back to the originating circumstances with our parents, we are likely to be dealing with surrogates and shadows. At whatever level the knot is loosened, however, the destructive energy in all the pictures will diminish in direct proportion to that picture's symbolic importance.

There is only one way to destroy a Stuck Picture: stop trying to be right. Stop taking a position in opposition to someone else's position. Let them be right (for them) so that you can stop putting energy into making them wrong. Go on to something more productive by taking responsibility for what is right *for you.* Other people represent our hopes and fears for ourselves. If we can face our fears through them, we can go on to lead much richer lives.

12.

What To Do About Losing

THE RIGHT/WRONG GAME can be very gratifying—as long as we are winning! Statistically, that can only be about 50% of the time. If you think you are beating the statistics, look at it this way: all negative emotions indicate that you are losing the game. If you don't want to feel miserable, you have got to start pulling yourself out of this game.

I want to give you an emotion-by-emotion analysis of what's going wrong in your game plan so that you can gain some insight into what is causing your particular problem. Then you can stop dealing with distress ineffectively at the effect, or physical, level and start getting your inner machine working properly. Overall, you should be building up your self-respect to the point where you can play the *really* exhilarating game of me-AND-you. Remember also that if you are experiencing the emotion, the problem lies with you. It is NEVER, NEVER, NEVER the other person. He or she is only highlighting an interior "dis-ease."

* * *

SELF-PITY is the stock in trade of the practicing victim. The practicing victim's viewpoint can arise from a general belief: "See how terrible life can be—and how admirable I am for enduring such misery!" It can arise from a Stuck Picture: "Good wives should serve their husbands."—covering a picture of one's own disobedience. Or it can simply be the victim's wish to make someone else wrong. "I'll pick up after him and then I'll tell him how bad it is to live with a slob." (I can't help but remember one friend's solution to this aggravation. She nailed all her husband's clothes to the floor. See what fun you can have if you don't play the right/wrong game!)

In any event, victims are caught in a dilemma. They cannot move to an aggressive mode of behavior without 1) changing a basic belief about life, 2) being willing to be "wrong" themselves, 3) allowing someone else to be right.

If you feel sorry for yourself find out what it is you wish to support. You will very soon come to a challenge to your pride—a pride in being right—about your astute observations concerning life, about your essential goodness, or about someone else's wrong behavior. At this point you will have to determine for yourself if you would rather be right *and a victim* of if it's okay to stop playing the right/wrong game. If you are making someone wrong—and you probably are—can you walk away from your opponent without collecting your pound of flesh? Can you let him off the mat? Keep asking yourself which is more important—making him pay or having to pay yourself by being victimized? If you persevere in these matters, you will reach a point where all you can do is laugh at the stupidity of the priorities you have set. At that point you have healed yourself of this particular problem because you are now free to make constructive decisions about how to better your circumstances. You are no longer playing ego games.

*   *   *

GRIEF is a form of self-pity. The loss of a loved one is terrible, indeed, but nonetheless we are still grieving for our personal loss. When we choose to be poor losers in the face of death we argue with life itself. We picture ourselves as the targets of misfortune and in that self-centeredness, we fail to respect the wishes of those who have chosen to die. The departed loved one, I can assure you, never had it so good. My father, who had a lovely sense of humor, told me (after his death) that if he had known it were going to be this good he would have done it a long time ago!

For many of us, mourning a death gives us an opportunity to release a general self-pity which would be unacceptable under normal conditions. A death can represent something we feel we have missed out on. Public figures and heroes for whom we grieve can provide this kind of focus. We see in their death the death of our own hopes and aspirations and grieve (for ourselves) accordingly.

Some grieve because they believe they would be disloyal if they didn't. Yet our misery does not honor the dead. In fact, it hampers them by making them anxious for our welfare. Our joy in having known them is the greatest honor we can bestow. Some grieve because the dead person suddenly becomes symbolic of all that is good and noble. This sudden ascent to perfection—a perfection which was very likely challenged in life—serves to shine the light of guilt upon ourselves. We remember with shame our sins of omission and commission in relation to the deceased. The real problem, therefore, is our guilt and not bereavement.

I once heard a minister say that a particular parishioner had not finished mourning her husband's death and therefore would be unable to participate in an excursion planned by the church. The death over which this woman grieved had taken place many months before but both the minister and the woman were locked into beliefs that grief takes a long time to experience, that grief is debilitating, and that it helps to indulge in grief until boredom stops the process. All these beliefs make the assumption that self-pity is a virtue. Of course, grief should never be suppressed, but we should find true cause, or the source of our self-pity, quickly and deal with that self-pity appropriately.

*   *   *

GUILT is the personal presumption of inadequacy in the game of right/wrong. It is the fear of being wrong. But again, remember that the belief in that inadequacy was placed in the analyzer by your own ego. If you feel guilty, you are experiencing your own inability to live up to your own rules. You must ask yourself some questions. "Why have I adopted this particular rule?" "If I changed the rules, who would be right that I am presently trying to make wrong?"

Remember that other people symbolize the critical portion of ourselves. If you feel guilty because you cheated on your diet, for instance, ask yourself why you *like* to feel guilty. Why do you make your critical self right and your functioning self wrong? What would you lose if the roles of the two selves were reversed, making the "cheater" right? *Either you haven't taken responsibility for making the rules or you haven't taken responsibility for breaking them.* You cannot feel guilty if you accept yourself as you are.

Day to day guilt can arise because we want to be considered unselfish (right). At the same time, we want to do things our way and that way we consider selfish (wrong). The problem is how to *look* good while *behaving* selfishly. As these are self-described attributes and you think there is a difference, it can't be done. Usually we decide in the other person's favor and then attempt to even the score by making him miserable for "forcing" (???) the decision upon us. "Alright! We'll go to Pepe's for dinner but you know how I hate Mexican food!" Such acquiescence is, as it is intended to be, a gift deprived of all generosity. It says, "If you won't let me win, I can still see to it that you regret you won."

If dining at Pepe's appeals to your friend, but not to you, you have two positive choices. You can refuse to go to Pepe's but you must then be willing to face your friend's possible displeasure. This is taking responsibility for your action. Or you can go to Pepe's recognizing that YOU decided to do this. This is also taking responsibility for your action. You see, happy people make choices. Unhappy people believe they have choices thrust upon them because they are not taking responsibility for what *they* are doing. Happy people also see to it that they have fun, no matter what they are doing because they know they "did it."

If you want out of this game, you must begin to change your rules. Stop expecting others to bolster your ego and stop trying to bolster theirs. Take care of yourself; let them take care of themselves. Respect your own needs and those needs will be respected by others. Mostly. If it happens that you lose a friend with this approach, you will know you never really had that friend in the first place. You only had someone who was using you to validate himself. That's not much of a friend.

*   *   *

JEALOUSY is a signal that the validation process by which we set such store isn't working. We decided, inappropriately, that our beloved could put us on a pedestal, making us feel lovable, cherished, sexually special, etc. Unfortunately, if he or she can put us on a pedestal, he or she can also remove us. When this pedestal is delivered to someone else's door, we have lost the game of winners and losers. We are losers in a game we ourselves set up.

In addition, fidelity has likely been either promised or implied. The beloved is clearly wrong by your set of rules but not by his (or hers). You must ask yourself how much of your jealous feelings go towards the beloved and how much towards the new interest. Who is to "blame?" If you blame your beloved, it is the rules you care about. If you blame the new interest, it is your validation you care about.

Sexual feelings are highly complex. We use sex to out-picture so many of our games. Anyone caught in a me-OR-you mental set more than likely uses sex as a power game in which vanquishing the partner—making him or her succumb to our "overpowering" attractiveness—provides the true satisfaction. Overt forms of this game can range from seduction to rape, though many play this game covertly using impotence, pre-ejaculation, sexual teasing which culminates in denial, or the withholding of orgasm to disappoint the partner. The psychological perception is, "See how powerful I am. I can withhold the prize and you can do nothing about it."

The purposeful stimulation of jealousy can be another ploy in the sexual game. But no matter what arouses jealousy, the feelings come because we feel inadequate to the occasion. We have lost our power base. Until we stop believing that power can be assigned to us by another, we will run the risk of pain. True power comes from within. And true love is played in the me-AND-you mode.

Sometimes our sense of betrayal and the ensuing jealousy is made more keen because we feel that we have sacrificed something in trying to make the relationship work. The belief is that we are owed something for all that we have done. Debts have no place in a relationship. Obliging a friend or mate by "making a sacrifice" (if only in your mind) means that you are playing a power game and want tribute. If you give, recognize that you give on your own behalf, perhaps even because you haven't the will to deny your gift.

*   *   *

ENVY is the feeling we have when someone else has what we wish for ourselves. It is different than jealousy in that jealousy is the fear of losing what we already have. Envy is bred of our fear of impotence. It is a statement that we cannot be effective in our own lives. We cannot get what we want. The good things of life come to those who expect them. They do not come to those who merely wish for them or even to those who deserve them. *Life is not fair* because it is not a system of punishment and reward as almost all religions teach us. *Life is based upon a system of out-pictured expectations*—GOOD AND BAD! If you allow yourself the power base which is yours by right, you need envy no one. When we abdicate this power base, we do so because we would prefer to play victim and make someone else wrong for his or her behavior.

*   *   *

ANGER comes in two forms. One arises from a sense of self-worth and the other from its absence. Positive anger is an aggressive response in the me-AND-you mode. It is quick, sudden, and therapeutic; it subsides quickly. This kind of anger might better be called high indignation and it is very creative. Like a thunderstorm, it clears the air and readjusts the environment. It is very positive, but because all anger is mistakenly considered negative, I mention it in our present discussion.

Most originating causes for anger are small and the response should also be small. When animals get angry, they start with warning signals appropriate to the offense given. A dog will give a low menacing growl which clearly states that you are proceeding in the wrong direction. Or a cat may suddenly stop purring and rake you with her claws. "Stop what you are doing," she says. We, too, should get angry in small and therapeutic doses as the need to point out direction arises. We should not suppress anger until it erupts in torrents.

Anger is a signal every bit as important as a smile and should be used on behalf of our welfare as well as the welfare of those around us. It is dishonest to send others false signals that all is well when it is not. Besides, our subterfuge fools no one. All of us can recognize anger by the tight little smile. What we probably can't figure out is what caused the offense. In particular, children suffer from the tight-little-smile ploy because, given their naivete, they do not know which of the two signals to follow.

The second kind of anger builds slowly. It is stored instead of expressed as each incident arises. Under the rules of your particular right/wrong game it is wrong to express anger even if you can't stop feeling it. Family rows which start over who gets to read the paper first and end in murder display the outer limits of this sort of behavior. It is my observation that most of us are sitting on a lot of anger because we believe that it's not nice to be angry. Yet without anger, we can become defenseless. As a simplified generalization, I would go so far as to say that anyone who has *any* health problem or "bad luck" in general has become the victim of his own anger. There is no such thing as an unexpressed emotion, remember, if we are intent upon not expressing it towards others it will be expressed towards ourselves.

If you are angry frequently—expressed or otherwise—you are playing the right/wrong game with those around you. You have set up the rules (in your head) and expect them to be followed. Before you can begin rooting out the problem, however, you must first determine if the rules are important or are they simply an opportunity to make someone wrong? My own impression is that chronically angry people are lying in wait to make someone—almost anyone—wrong. This means that not only is there a Stuck Picture (See Chapter 11) but what is stuck is the right/wrong game itself. Only you can decide if the aggravation, the lack of friends, the strain on the family and the work place, a chronic physical condition, etc., is worth the self-assigned trophy. If they aren't, try living by a new rule: live and let live.

On the other hand, it may really be someone else's conduct which is bugging you. After you have located the Stuck Picture you must come to understand that while you are free to shape your life in any way you wish, you are not free to determine this for another no matter how reasonable and positive your suggestions and hopes for the other might be. Some people are determined to be self-destructive (or infantile or self-centered, etc.) and therefore they take actions which are not in their best interests (or mature or generous). You must acknowledge this in *good will* and give them rein to be themselves. They may change but not be-

cause you wish it or because you know better how they should behave. They are already doing the best they know how, given their
own beliefs.

There is also the distinct possibility that your rules are the kind
of rules which *should* be in place. We are social beings, after all,
and must observe the recognized arrangements in dealing with
each other. You may be more than justified in your anger. But
then, if you are involved with someone who is too self-destructive
(or infantile or self-centered, etc.) why do you stick around? Trying to be a good guy? Trying to be right? Trying to win? I give you
then the spoils of Pyrrhus who declared, "One more such victory
and we are lost!"

*   *   *

HATE is self-loathing turned outward. We have worked hard
to overcome our supposed deficiencies. One way of stamping out
an undesirable trait is to turn a fear of it into a hate of it. Naturally
enough, we hate in others what we hate in ourselves. Besides, no
one likes to be forced to a diet of cottage cheese and carrot sticks
unless the man who is pigging out on ice cream can be made to pay
for his "sins." We hate to see others enjoy the privileges we forbid
ourselves. Bigots, religious and political fanatics of every description, even those who bristle unduly at the mention of a particular
subject like smoking or homosexuality are scorning in others what
they fear (and hence forbid) in themselves. They play the right/
wrong game. Feeling compelled to do right, they wish to force
others to their same discomfort. Hate is a very involving emotion.
Haters are very involved with what they hate. It is ruling them.
What they hate lies beneath a Stuck Picture.

I once heard an excerpt from a talk-show having to do with
prayer in the schools. The caller said that anyone who didn't believe in God (her God, of course!) should be denied citizenship.
Well, now! There is someone who is having a great deal of trouble

with her own godliness (as she perceives those qualities). She evinces this by hating the godless. She has tried to extinguish these unwanted attributes within herself but it has been very difficult and the fear that they will resurface is never very far from her mind. It seems only right to her that others who have not made the same effort suffer some sort of punishment. As compensation for her efforts, she at least wants to be right. Imagine finding out you were wrong after inflicting such a brow-beating on yourself!

We can always find what we hate in ourselves by noticing what really angers us about others. In all cases we are dealing with Stuck Pictures. What we hate in others are the feared truths in our own belief systems. We despise the lazy because we fear our own laziness. We despise smokers because they are getting away with something we had to give up in order to be right. We despise members of a different race or religion because they are not conforming to a mold we struggled to fit into ourselves. We despise warmongers because we fear our own aggression. Hate (intolerance) is an ugly emotion to have within your system. It is very self-destructive. It literally eats away and poisons your own body. The hate of others is far less harmful to those you hate than it is to you. I urge you to work hard at digging out and dissolving the Stuck Picture which holds such beliefs in place. You are playing the right/wrong game at a dangerous level.

*   *   *

ANXIETY is a form of fear, as are all negative emotions. While it is not so apt to be associated directly with the right/wrong game, it does reflect an unhelpful negative attitude. Anxiety arises when an outcome is unknown but the worst is imagined. (Do you remember what the imagination can create?) When we are in the midst of a terrifying situation, we have no time to think. We have only time for action. It is only when we have nothing better to do that we begin to anticipate an outcome by building a worst-case scenario. As long as we do not know what the outcome is going to be we should not increase our present misery by dwelling upon, and hence reinforcing, that negative by giving it additional power to create itself. One of my father's favorite quotations was, "I am an old man and I have had many worries but most of them have never happened!" Hold the thought. It's just possible that life may not be as bad as you think.

Many times anxiety is a self-imposed protection against optimism. We reason that the drop is shorter from a state of anxious apprehension to disappointment. It isn't. It just seems that way because we have taken it in steps. Disappointment and even tragedy can be dealt with when it comes. Dealing with it *before* it comes only makes it more likely to happen.

There are a host of other negative emotions—loneliness, frustration, vulnerability—to mention a few. In one way or another these feelings arise from a sense of personal inadequacy. In a setting of winners and losers, these are the feelings of losers. If you feel like a loser, you need to ask yourself what you *win* by losing. To whom do you wish to play victim? Or are you saying that life itself is brutalizing? Each of us lives his own picture of life. This is the opportunity afforded by having a physical body. Think of life as an art class. We can daub away at our canvasses in muddy, unpleasant colors or we can aspire to a masterpiece. Remember, we do not ask that Michaelangelo be right. We marvel only at his self-expression.

13.

Ends and Means

EACH AND EVERY ONE OF US IS ENTITLED TO ALL THE JOY AND HAPPINESS AND HEALTH AND MATERIAL ADVANTAGE THAT THE BEST OF US CAN ENVISION. It is our inheritance. But it cannot be forced on us without denying the freedom of choice. The good life is voluntary. If you do not have an occupation which brings you joyous satisfaction, if you are not nestled into a gloriously loving network of other people, if you do not have a standard of living which allows you your wishes, if you do not enjoy excellent health, and if you are not in love with living, you are cheating yourself. You are settling for less that is your due and you are playing victim wherever an optimum has not materialized. You are out-picturing disrespect for yourself. You are playing at being a victim of life when life should be rich in its rewards. *A life richly rewarding is your right!*

But there is something odd about rights. They are self-assigned. They belong only to those who believe they are entitled to them. In a cosmic system such as ours, a system founded on freedom, such rights cannot be conferred. They must be assumed. This is why waiting for a messiah is such an incredibly sad expectation.

Before we explore some techniques for changing our life patterns at the causal level, I think an overview would be helpful. Each of us is on a path—would you believe the same path? We are trying to achieve the good life for ourselves—and possibly others. Too many of us think the good life arrives with a whopping big mortgage and children who take ballet and play on Little League teams. Not exactly. The good life arrives when our hearts and minds are in love with the experience of living. In most cases this demands a lot of mind changes, and this is the worst request anyone can make of us. Primarily the good life demands getting out of the right/wrong game by facing the fear of losing. It's a lot to ask.

Perhaps I should call this chapter pre-surgery counselling. It sets goals, establishes requirements and explains the steps to recovery. It provides a focus so that you can marshall your expectations, understand your responsibilities, and mark your progress. Too many of us sit by passively waiting for life to offer something better. I must say it again: life is an outer picture of an interior mind-set. It *cannot* picture what is not there to be pictured any more than we can aim a camera at a tenement and expect a snapshot of the Taj Mahal when we get back the developed film. Want the Taj Mahal? *You* will have to built it yourself. The Creating Cosmos cannot respond to passiveness.

Life owes us nothing—nor does anyone else. Life gives us the opportunity to do for ourselves. That, in itself, is an inestimable gift for it gives us the chance to fulfill our own expectations and set our sights as high (or as low) as we wish. Expecting life (in the form of others) to offer rewards without our active involvement in the process of the achievement of those rewards makes us psychologically weak. We are thrown into a position of dependence upon those others. Yet the enjoyment of life depends directly on a feeling of self-sufficiency, a feeling that—come what may—we know we can take care of ourselves.

Self-sufficiency means much more than having enough money. It means being able to rely on ourselves to affect positively all aspects of life. Women by the thousands are waiting for a man to come along to "make them happy." They do not understand that happiness is self-initiated. Essentially what these women want is a man who will provide a purpose for living. But this begs the question. Such arrangements do not provide self-sufficiency but dependency (and fear) because the very guts of life—its purpose—is supposedly to be provided by someone else. Children grow up and mates die (or even walk away) and if they have previously provided "the purpose for living" for a woman thus bereft, that woman has made her life happiness conditional upon the acts of others.

It's nice to be protected from what we fear, but protection doesn't really make the fear go away. We need to dissolve the fear by tapping into our own power. Finding Mr. Right or being financially or physically dependent only serves to demonstrate the effectiveness of our "helper." It does nothing for our own power base.

Health is another area in our lives in which we, as a population, are increasingly surrendering our autonomy. More and more, it is popular to "put ourselves under the care of a doctor." I will have much more to say about matters of health in subsequent chapters, but for now, perhaps you can begin to see what becoming doctor- or drug-dependent does for your sense of *self*-reliance. All health problems—in one way or another—are created by feelings of vulnerability or impotence. Handing over the responsibility for our health to a doctor only exacerbates the original problem, indicated by the tremendous rise in the number of those needing health care.

The intent of these observations on self-reliance is to bring into finer focus your own non-responsibility. Unless you are reading this book out of idle curiousity, you are reading it in the hope of improving your life. Towards this end, your first commitment *has* to be a clear understanding that IT IS UP TO YOU! Sorry about that! Now . . . having just lost the interest of 70% of my readers, let me go on to remind everyone that all of us are incredibly powerful. That means we *do not need* to wait upon others. Knowing this we no longer have the right to complain.

What has been missing from human experience is a true knowledge of that awesome power we have to conduct our lives and the effect that power has on the webbings between ourselves and others. That power draws kindred souls in towards us to do our bidding in either helpful or destructive ways. Ignorant of this power, we establish institutions, not to bring personal power into its true fruition, but to protect us from its imagined absence. We have been educated to indulge our fears and humble our strengths. From politics to social etiquette, from international agreements to love affairs, we demand that our self-assigned frailties be compensated, our imagined impotence be acknowledged, and our fears allayed. Thus it is that the myth of our impotence is perpetuated and the fact of our personal power obscured. Only in a state of fierce autonomy can we reach out with total compassion—with love. We need that love. We cannot exist in a Nuclear Age if we do not come to acknowledge that it must be—from here on out—a me-AND-you world, a world founded on transcendent purpose, a world founded on love. And that means your love. You can help your world community best by becoming a self-actualizing lover.

*   *   *

We come now to what I think of as the rings of reality. These rings are directly keyed to personal self-confidence and self-respect. The more self-confidence and self-respect we have the higher will be the ring of reality in which we find ourselves. The difficulty is that we are likely to get stuck in one of the lower rings unless we appreciate that something else lies beyond. This is because the belief systems we adopt as our truths create a reality which seems to be implacably real. The reality we create (and live in) appears as a factual reality. We are therefore likely to stop at a truth or a belief which is, in this context, only a half-truth. This is okay on a temporary basis. The object of all inner exploration is movement towards a goal of self-understanding. Every step we take in that direction is of benefit because every step will increase self-sufficiency and in turn create a new vantage point from which to find higher truths. My advice, however, is to push against any inclination to stop along the way. Enjoy where you are on this inward trip, but recognize, too, that inward possibility is infinite.

For the purposes of making my explanations of the different realities more graphic, let's call the perspective of the first reality that of the dependent child, the second that of the adolescent who is coming of age, the third the adult who has matured, and the fourth the senior years of wisdom. This is only an analogy. None of us lives exclusively within one reality. It is perhaps a matter of percentages. We all have our strengths and weaknesses. We fall behind in some areas of our lives and are well ahead in others. Many children are born wise and many oldsters are victims of their dependence. Let's look then at each ring of reality in greater detail.

The first reality focuses around the perception that we are the victims of life rather than the masters and creators of it. In this reality, life is something which is "done" to us. The expectations established by our beliefs are very low and there is usually much emotional pain and physical suffering. Life is to be endured "in quiet desperation" if not in actual tragedy. We are losers in the game of winners and losers.

Usually we enter the second reality when the press of being a victim finally challenges what little self-respect we have. We revolt. We get angry—sometimes very angry. And this is good. Such anger means that some portion of our self-respect has been engaged. Culturally, this reality is the stage of revolution. It means peasant against tyrant, labor against management, black against white, etc. On a personal level, it means having enough self-respect to stand up to those we hold responsible for making our lives miserable. This is primarily the reality of our culture—a culture which externalizes blame. We mean to be winners in the game of winners and losers.

By the time we attain the third reality, we have accepted responsibility for the course of events which make up our lives. We find the cause of our problems within ourselves instead of in the actions and responses of others. This book is principally about attaining this third reality and looking forward to the promise of the next one. It requires great personal strength to enter this third reality. For one thing, this reality is not culturally acknowledged. It goes against all social indoctrination to find "blame" in oneself. Not only is this reality unfamiliar, but we will find no social validation for accepting the truths of this reality. For another thing, we have gotten into the messes we are enduring because "blame" is the last thing on earth (literally) we wish to accept. We have perhaps spent hundreds of lifetimes kidding ourselves that we are blameless because being wrong is so fearsome. It is in this third reality that we must begin to face those fears. Entering this reality takes real guts because of those fears. We will return therefore to the subject of fear as soon as we have looked at the pay-off—the next reality.

The fourth reality lies on the other side of fear. Faced, our fears appear for what they really are—imaginative constructs of our own making. In this reality we are at last strong enough to express real compassion and love both for ourselves and for others. This is the reality called happiness, inner peace, a state of grace, etc. It is heaven on earth—as all physical experience should be. Best of all, it is such glorious fun because such nice things happen "unexpectedly."

What lies beyond this fourth reality I do not know nor can I imagine. Such is the limitation of a particular reality. Its boundaries can only be broken by the imagination yet the imagination itself is limited by the reality. It seems to me, however, that from this fourth reality all things are possible. Where those possibilities take the traveller, I cannot guess, unless it be towards the spontaneous expression of ecstasy.

*   *   *

Fear arises from a belief in impotence. And impotence creates fear. It is an unending circle which can only be broken if we stop running from our fears and face them. A friend of mine dreamed a boa constrictor had coiled and recoiled around her body. She was terrified, particularly as the head of the snake was right in front of her and staring her in the face. She was searching frantically for help of any kind when a wise man suddenly appeared. He told her that the only way out of her mortal danger was to kiss the snake. This is what we must all do eventually. We must kiss the snake so that the fears which bind us to our miseries will dissolve.

Facing fear—or kissing the snake—is the worst task we shall ever have to undertake. None of us would willingly do so unless the pay-off for doing so were very great. Such interior muckraking makes sense only when we come to recognize what terrible things can happen if those fears are allowed to remain unresolved. Each of us must therefore first address the question: which is worse—dredging up old fears or suffering the current misfortunes which plague our lives? If these misfortunes are not particularly unpleasant, don't bother with old fear. It isn't worth it. You won't be sufficiently motivated in any case.

I know of only two ways to deal with fear. One is to enter directly into a state of fearlessness by believing to the point of knowingness (See Chapter 17) that we have nothing to fear and that the cause of all fear is self-inspired. An undeviating faith in an all-caring God or a personal savior like Jesus can provide this focus. While this can be very beneficial, it does not address the true source of our fears which is our perceived personal weakness. In effect we say, "If I don't let go of God's hand, I'm okay because He can do something for me I cannot do for myself." It is a prop.

As long as it is in place it will work (like any hypnotic spell) but sooner or later we must come to understand our own divine power. To believe that only God possesses divine power denigrates our own power base. In effect we still fear for ourselves, if not our circumstances. We can also achieve a state of fearlessness without a belief in God but it is a gigantic step in the assimilation of cosmic truth. It requires more understanding that most of us can achieve immediately.

The second approach is to take the circumstances at hand and trace them back to a specific fear and face that fear until it has been de-energized and seen for what it is—a silly invention of our own minds. The next chapter deals with this approach.

14.

In Search of Cause

IT IS DIFFICULT to give exact directions or make precise equations between a specific causal belief and a particular circumstance because we are such distinct individuals. We are each the proverbial snowflake. We use our own symbols and formulate our own designs in the expression of them. One person may prefer to express his problems in his body while another may "attack" his automobile or his bank account. Even so, both the automobile and the bank account will have different symbolic meanings for each person.

For instance, at one point I was having considerable trouble with my car. Why, I wondered? A friend suggested a car was considered a sex symbol by many people. Well, not for me, I discovered. *My* car turned out to be an umbilical cord, symbolically. Its primary function in my life was to take me out to get necessities as my needs arose. When I found this out I also discovered by going back in my journals that whenever mother came to town (or I *thought* she was coming to town!) my car stopped running. Unfaced fears about mother's general unreliability out-pictured themselves symbolically. On the surface, I looked forward, as any adult child might, to a visit from my mother. Underneath, a little girl's unfaced fears were all being highlighted by the anticipated visit. Because I denied these fears on a conscious level, the energy they generated had no choice but to replicate those fears in a way we choose to call symbolic. In my case I feared I would be betrayed by my mother, my umbilical cord, my life-line, my car. And I was! This is why we must all become aware of our own symbolism for I doubt that your car is an umbilical cord *to you.*

The true difficulty in finding a belief is that we do not perceive beliefs to be beliefs, but to be facts. In searching out the cause of our difficulties, we are likely to skip right over these facts as givens: "There is a prejudice against women in the market place," "The older you get, the more likely you are to get sick," "He shouldn't have ripped me off," "What she said to me was rude and insulting." It is therefore of great help to state every fact within a complex of circumstances as a belief. "*I believe that* there is a prejudice against women in the market place," "*I believe that* he shouldn't have ripped me off," etc.

The next step is to understand that all out-pictured circumstances are circumstances which, considering our beliefs, are more desirable than any other. This is difficult when those very circumstances are making us so miserable, but the fact remains that were the situation to be changed, it would run counter to a belief we wish to cherish and uphold. The most direct approach to this hurdle is to state all conditions as if they were conditions we found desirable and then to find out why they indeed are such.

In order to help you find your own causal beliefs, I'm going to give you three specific examples so that you can examine the process with an eye to translating the routine to your own experiences. The first two examples concern general circumstances and the third concerns a specific incident. Specific incidents can be much more productive because the focus is much sharper. They reproduce the belief so precisely. All we need to do is read the message correctly. The disadvantage is that unless we are quick about it, the nuances of a given situation are likely to recede from conscious memory.

In the first example Jerry was forced (under the rules of the game) to explain his rather miserable circumstances this way: "*I believe* that it is desirable to be in debt. *I believe* that it is best to be too poor to make financial ends meet." The question is *why*, because notwithstanding what he found "desirable," he was terribly frightened by what was happening to him and the financial mess he was making of his life.

Pauline, in the second example, *believes* that it is *desirable* to experience a series of meaningless love affairs and to forsake having a husband and babies. Again, the question is why, considering that this lack is causing her despair.

When we describe the circumstances as harshly as this, we are already beginning to take charge. We can begin to see ourselves as creators even though we may be creating what we don't like instead of what we do. We can also begin to face the problem at hand in a way that lamentations for our general misery can never do.

Now we can begin to search for the operative beliefs which are creating these circumstances. Like investigators at the scene of a crime, we must untangle the puzzle. Again, I think it helps to divide up the assignments within the mind so that one self answers the questions with as much honesty and emotional expression as possible and another self punches away with unrelenting and critical perseverance so that the emotional and "human" self does not get off the hook. The object is to discover the Wipe Out Picture which has become stuck. If you can no longer remember a particular scene (picture), invent one that corresponds to the feeling tones you are finding in your memory. "I don't remember that my mother ever told me that I was ugly, but I always understood that this was what she thought." Make that remembered sentiment into a reality (because that is what it truly is) by inventing a scene which would have described what you experienced if that scene had actually taken place. This is not cheating for it *is* going on in your mind and for the mind, what it imagines is *real* for it, and therefore real for you.

*   *   *

So now, let's take up Jerry's story.

Jerry was in debt. He couldn't hold a job for more than a few months. When things got too bleak, he got his father to bail him out of his predicament but his father was getting fed up. Besides, Jerry hated the humiliation and he wanted out of his game.

"You are expressing dependence on your father. You are also expressing a belief in your inability to take care of yourself. The question is why is it better to have your father take care of you than take care of yourself? What do you gain? Can you think of an occasion when your father wiped you out—left you powerless?"

"I can think of many, but the one that is most vivid is the time Dad said I had no rights unless he gave them to me. We were discussing my bike and I said something like, 'Well, it's my bike! I can do what I want with my own bike!' My father shot back, 'That bike is not yours. It's mine. Everything you think you own belongs to me because you are a minor and therefore you'll do as I say!' I was stunned. I felt—yes—wiped out."

"Let's back up a minute. First, you were protecting yourself in the right/wrong game. You wanted to be right about your bike. But your father did an end run and took away your base for being right. The game shifted from right/wrong to winners and losers. These same pictures are manifesting today because you didn't fully experience either being wrong or losing. What did you think at that time which would make you both right and a winner?"

"Nothing. I was totally bewildered."

"Go back to that moment and *imagine* an emotional solution, not a solution which you might invent now that you are more mature. Get mad."

"I'll tell you what I would want to do. I'd say, 'Okay, if that's the way you want it, that's the way you'll have it. I'll show you how mean you are. I'll make you wrong yet. I'll make you pay for—God, how literal can I get?" Jerry interrupted himself.

"Has it been worth it?"

"No. It's a stupid game. And yet I still feel wiped out by that jerk."

"Pretend that your father was not your father but a small boy like yourself. Imagine that you were playing at his house and that he angrily said you couldn't play with his toys anymore because they weren't yours. What would your reaction have been?"

"I would have thought he was nuts. *Of course* they were his toys but if he wanted me to play with him at his house, he would *have* to share. I would have thought he was being a spoiled brat and probably wouldn't play with him again unless I had to. Then I'd force conditions to our playing."

"Can you think of your father as a spoiled brat?"

"Yes, and I feel sorry for him once I get into neutral about the whole thing. It's going to take some work—staying in neutral—but at least I know what to work on."

*   *   *

Pauline was 36. She had lots of boy friends but none of her relationships lasted very long. She put it this way: "I want the ones I can't have and I don't want the ones I can." Still, she said she wanted to be married and have children. The question is what does she gain from her present situation that she would lose if she were married? Who would be right and thereby make her wrong?

"What do you see as the biggest disadvantage in marriage?"

"I suppose it would be that I couldn't play the field anymore. I like that option. It really boosts my ego to turn a man on."

"Who told you that you were unattractive?"

"No one needed to. I was a real dumpy kid. When my father divorced my mother—I was thirteen—I must have weighed 150 pounds. Worst of all I was what my Mom called boy crazy, and being fat wasn't helping me a bit."

"What did your father's departure say to you?"

"It was no big deal. I went off to play tennis after I was told."

"Is that your reaction now when a man leaves you?"

"Not exactly! I cry a lot and feel absolutely miserable. I feel so utterly worthless and unattractive. All I can think about is how to get him back or how to find someone else as fast as I can so I won't feel so shitty."

"Let's pretend that if you had been willing to experience your father's leaving, this is what you would have felt then too. Give yourself over to those feelings—just pretending, of course. Now tell me what his subliminal statement is to you and what your reaction to that subliminal statement is."

"His statement to me is that I am unattractive to a man. And my response is not only to deny it, but to prove to him that he is wrong."

"The feared truth then is that you are a wash-out sexually, and the covering picture is that you are sexually provocative. Do you see that if you did get married, you couldn't go on proving yourself anymore? Your interest in men is not so much in loving them but in using them to make your father's imagined statement wrong."

"Well, how do I change that? I really do want to move ahead with my life."

"You will have to face your fear of being unloveable, unattractive, unsexual—however you wish to describe it in its worst terms. You will have to experience emotionally what it feels like to be a dumpy kid who wants boys and can't get them. When you've done this and come to know that all these qualities which you presently think will make or break you can do *neither,* then you will not need men anymore. You will then be free to love them. Or even one!"

*   *   *

Because I can only correct in myself what I know to be amiss, I try to give careful attention to anything untoward which turns up in my life. I take such events seriously and do what I can, as the occasions arise, to discover my inner thought processes and to clean up the "dirty pictures" which are being out-pictured in these unpleasant events. If you are quick about it, you can find the specific belief right on the surface because somewhere in the immediate past you have succumbed to feelings which spell out a particular belief.

The problem is that these moods are usually fleeting and are apt to go all but unnoticed consciously. They are unacknowledged, which is exactly why they must express themselves covertly. If you wait any length of time, therefore, it is likely that the connection between mood and event will escape conscious awareness. I keep a journal for this reason. Even so I find that it has only limited value because I don't record moment to moment moods. For those who do, you may be in great luck. Expressed on paper, these moods may not have to express themselves as events. However, I do record what's going on in my life and I can frequently reconstruct the moods attendant to these events. For this reason, I recommend a journal of some sort for anyone seriously determined to improve his or her experiences. If you do not catch these moods as you experience them, you can at least see, after the fact, how they were building themselves towards an unpleasant occurrence.

One such event happened to me only last week. It was a small "accident" but it is an excellent example of the symbolic meaning of such "accidents" and of how an unacknowledged emotion can manifest in physical reality. What impresses me is the accuracy of the out-pictured symbolism as it relates to the interior thought. Every fact of a particular thought seems to be there physically. This means that if you can focus on a specific incident immediately, you can see clearly a detailed picture of what is bothering you. You do not have to fill in with a lot of guess work. It is all there on the display screen and you have only to read it correctly. And, of course, deal with the problem your inquiry presents!

I was stung by a bee. She crawled up my pant leg as I was watering the garden, and with no warning that she was even present, she stung me badly. The sting caused such a swelling that I limped for two days. I particularly like this example because we all know that getting stung by a bee is getting stung by a bee and nothing more, right? But because I believe otherwise, I began to ask myself what on earth was going on in the recesses of my mind that had forced this to happen. The answer was certainly not obvious. I felt happy, productive, and serene. What then would cause this stinging pain? Did the very inflamed swelling indicate I felt angry about something? What about the limp? Was the Stuck Picture which had created this "accident" crippling? The incident had been a ghastly surprise. What did that signify? Was there one Stuck Picture which had all the elements of surprise, anger, pain, and crippledness?

It was then that I remembered the Three Day Rule. The Three Day Rule is the most useful tool I know about when it comes to finding causes for these kinds of sudden events. Years ago, my father passed along a study someone had done on a 36½ hour cycle in trauma. The man claimed (and I have since amply verified) that there is a lag of 36½ hours, or multiples of that figure, between an initiating trauma and its "aftershocks." A trauma will behave as if it were a pebble thrown into a pond and produce outward ripples which create similar events every 36½ hours until the energy from such a trauma is finally expended. The only trouble is that 36½ hours back from a specific event, I was more than likely to have been asleep. I was quite prepared to believe that my dream material at that moment had been most relevant to the event at hand but it didn't help much because I have very poor dream recall.

However, by doubling the cycle (as the man suggested) and by going back two ripples, or 73 hours, I could see some very interesting correlations between widely separated events. So now, I ask those suffering from almost any untoward event if they can remember back 3 days to a circumstance which, had they been a little boy or girl, would have wiped them out or made them cry. It has never failed to produce results for a person willing to explore such possibilities.

At first, they usually maintain that nothing happened; they drew a blank. Then a sheepish look comes over their faces. "No, wait a minute. That was the day my boss got angry at me," or "My husband and I had a big fight."

Sometimes it is possible to trace a whole series of unpleasant events as they build, timed by this 36½ hour cycle and its doubles. I have found, however, that the exact timing is apt to get out of whack after a while. It serves only as an approximation. Perhaps there are other cycles intervening. In any event, it is a magnificent tool. Try it the next time you get a cold. Three days (73 hours) before the serious onset of your cold, you will find an incident which momentarily defeated you and which you manfully rose above. You were wiped out and chose to ignore it consciously. It seems to take this long for the immune system to register vulnerability and physically present immune deficiency. Because of the delay between cause and effect, it suggests a little judicious "cleaning out" at the end of each day might prevent much in the way of physical ailments. I seldom get colds anymore but if one threatens I can stop it immediately by using the Three Day Rule to explore the real source of my difficulty. My colds don't last 7 days (or even a week!); they last about 15 minutes.

So what happened three days (73 hours) before I was stung by the bee? Seventy-three hours earlier made it 9:30 Monday morning. Suddenly I remembered. My God! That was the hour Fred had called to tell me Ann had died in her sleep the night before. Ann was a mutual friend we had both just seen. She had been in fine health as far as anyone knew, and now he was reporting her death. The news was a nasty shock. It had reminded me of my mother's equally sudden death only a year before. Mother had taken her own life at the age of 82, fearing her approaching invalidism. "I'm running a nursing home for one," she had once grumbled. Everything about her death had been a shock of immense proportions to me.

But what was it that particularly distressed me now? After some careful thinking, I put it most closely to feeling betrayed. I felt in some illogical way that I should have had some warning to prepare myself. These things just shouldn't be sprung on me (like a surprise bee sting?). Suddenness made me feel powerless. I felt victimized in some way. I thought about betrayal for awhile. But of course! The Big Betrayal was mother's sudden departure when I was 7 years old. I had even said to my brother when he called to tell me the terrible news, "She's already left me once. Why did she have to do this twice to me?"

On the occasion of the Big Betrayal (the Wipe Out Picture) mother had brought us East from California, presumably to be reunited with my father who had preceded us. We were indeed reunited with Dad, but when Dad was in place, so to speak, it turned out that mother was going to leave.

Because of the bee sting, I was forced, once again, to look at this picture of mother's "treachery" from yet another angle. It seemed to me that I had trusted mother (and Ann and garden wildlife, etc.) and that in return for my trust, mother had forced me to accept the unacceptable. I was betrayed. And there was absolutely nothing I could do about it. What I wanted was time—time to withdraw my trust, for that was what was at stake. I shouldn't have trusted her because that trust made me vulnerable.

"But if we can't trust others, how can we function?" I asked myself vehemently. "Trust is just something which has to be!"

"Now wait a minute," I continued. "You can't function? Do you mean to say that you can't function by yourself? No wonder you feel powerless if that is what you believe. Trusting others should have nothing to do with it. Trusting yourself is the way to reconstruct that belief."

I had blamed mother for my emotional crippledness most of my life. Now I was looking at the Wipe Out Picture as a betrayal of trust. Along with great pain, I had indeed been angry. But I could also see that if I had been willing to trust myself I would have grieved my mother's going, but I wouldn't have been wiped out.

I cannot stress strongly enough that the universe has been founded on the endowment of each physical manifestation with its own power over its own destiny. Any belief which runs athwart this fact is some form of a lie. When searching for high ground after you have found the belief that is causing you trouble, you must take that belief and turn it around until *you* are the source of power. The new belief will then conform to Truth. In other words, a very destructive conclusion to the bee sting episode would have been, "Okay, so now I'll never trust anyone again!" The original error we make is *always* to give away our self-determination by blaming, and we can only correct that error by taking responsibility for our faulted view of the world. All fear is, therefore, inappropriate and unnecessary. Incidentally, now when I work in my garden among the bees, I ask myself if there is anything I should feel "stung" about. If there isn't, I work on, fearless of being hurt.

*   *   *

The most fertile ground for self-discovery lies in our relationships with both our parents and our children. Both generations are apt to reflect our weaknesses and our strengths. It is our weaknesses which get us into trouble and those weaknesses are apt to be exacerbated by both parents and children alike. Not only do they punch our buttons, but they are likely to express our own fears in what appears to be a magnified form.

What bothers us about our parents and our children is not so much their failings but our expectations in their perfection. Until we can love them for who and what they are, we should be investigating our own demands both upon them and upon ourselves.

Getting back to Stuck Pictures will almost inevitably take us back to parental problems. But children too can be a constant reminder that we are not on course. The Infant Terrible may signal our own willingness to play the victim. The adolescent's growing need for independence may confront our own fears of that condition. His burgeoning sexuality may arouse our own unresolved anxieties. His inadequacies in adult life are likely to be our (self-described) inadequacies, not so much because he "inherited" them but because we describe them as such. What distresses us in our parents and our children is what distresses us in ourselves.

Positive solutions are more likely to be achieved with children if we grow up ourselves, for we tend in our children what needs tending in us. Children, I think, keep us very humble. We get our lives pretty much in order, we believe we are making good progress, and then along comes a child and his problems which sends us into spirals of anxiety on his behalf and we are back to square one. Benjamin Spock never mentioned this, did he?

*   *   *

Let's re-cap the process of finding cause so that you have the clearest possible guidelines for your own investigations.

1) Any troublesome condition which exists more or less permanently indicates that you are operating from a false belief concerning the human experience. It may have to do with a lack of positive expectation ("Let's face it! Life is an unending struggle."). It may have to do with an enculterated belief which denigrates the human condition ("Sexual feelings are animal feelings."). It may have to do with right and wrong, winners and losers. In all cases it is more than likely that a picture has become stuck because the ego believes its own false truths yet cannot accept their implications.

2) All "facts" are beliefs. State them as beliefs, not facts. They

will seem less solid that way.

3) The condition you are experiencing is the condition you prefer to the ideal situation. The object of the hunt is to find out why and to see if you would like to change the rules by which you have chosen to live.

4) The guilt picture or the wipe out picture is exactly duplicated by your present external circumstances. You are coping with this current problem in exactly the same inappropriate way that you used in the past. Nothing has changed but the characters in your play. You are Stuck!

5) The problem is created by a belief in contradiction to the laws of the cosmos. The solution you have chosen is also in contradiction to those laws. That is why you are experiencing discomfort. If you were on track—if your beliefs were in cosmic harmony—you would be in a state of joy. In other words, you fear something which is not real except in your head and your solutions follow from your false premise.

6) Don't go through the process intellectually. This is an emotional problem, not an intellectual one. The object is to *experience out* the emotion which is blocking a positive life experience. You have to *use up* your old emotions. Think of it as an abcess which must be drained. Simply noting intellectually that it exists doesn't do that.

7) My abbreviated examples make the search look easy. It isn't. Digging into a fear takes great patience and fortitude. Go at your own pace knowing that every confrontation with your feared truth will improve your external life proportionally. And don't belabor the process. Save soul-searching for miserable moments. Enjoy life between those moments. This will give you a reservoir of strength which will make you even better at facing fears when the next time comes around.

8) Remember that you are in fear because you feel insufficient unto yourself. This is false. Strive for anger, particularly if you are

dealing with a wipe out picture. Anger gets you beyond the stage of impotence, of playing victim. It signifies the return of self-respect. But remember also that the true culprit is not the person at whom you feel angry, but a belief of your own which puts you in a humbled position.

9) When you have found the belittling belief, change it to a positive one which returns your God-given power to where it belongs—to yourself.

10) If you begin to feel guilty about the griefs you may have caused others—don't! It takes two to play these games. Others have lessons to learn too. You may wish to acknowledge your less-than-ideal behavior but don't go into a *mea culpa* over your fresh appraisal of past events.

11) Life is a process. There is no place of destination. Enjoy the process because that is all there is.

15.

Beliefs Which Undermine Health

I F THE BODY is the temple of the soul, we, as a culture, worship in fear. Not only are we afraid of how our bodies look and how we adorn them, but we fear that if we do not take meticulous care of them, they are likely to fall into untimely and hopeless disrepair. Said a bit differently, we do not trust our bodies to know how to maintain their own health. That's a terrible indictment! How would you feel if someone said that to you about your own area of expertise? And yet, if you hold almost any of our culturally accepted beliefs about the process of health, this is what you are saying to your body.

If you take vitamins, have a list of foods which you shouldn't eat, exercise out of a sense of duty, see your doctor for a regular check-up, or invest in health insurance, you buy the notion that maintaining health is possible only under safely controlled conditions. You also believe that at any moment something terrible may go wrong with your body and most assuredly something will go wrong in the future unless you are very, very careful. As I've already said, you do not trust your body.

My guess is that something like 80% of all health problems in this country are due solely to the destructive beliefs we hold about health, the body, and the genesis of illness. The fact is that none of us needs to be sick except as we are unable to develop a trust in our bodies and their ability to maintain health naturally. Developing that trust is not easy when our entire ethos conspires against such faith, but I can assure you, the rewards can be enormous if such a faith is fostered.

Let's begin to build such confidence by making the following statement: *the body is functioning perfectly at all times!* If the body is expressing disorder—from congenital conditions to the common cold—it is because—for one reason or another—it has been commanded to do so. Therefore, if we change the commands, we can change the conditions. (Advanced necrosis, amputation, and extreme trauma where time is of the essence are the only exceptions which occur to me. In these cases the body's ability to recover has been exceeded by the circumstances.) I recognize that this may be a pretty big statement to swallow, particularly if a doctor has told you that your problem is incurable. Remember, however, that "incurable" relates only to the doctor's skills, not to the actual breadth of possibility.

In one way or another, any physical *dis*-ease is a symptom of self-described vulnerability. Vulnerability originates in a belief that there is a power external to the self which is greater than the self. Therefore, any belief which discredits personal power and re-assigns that power to another agent invites *dis*-ease. Unfortunately, almost all our beliefs about health are based on the assumption that power over these matters is beyond our direct control. Germs, bacteria, viruses, toxic chemicals, etc., control our health. Human efforts to *restore* health, once it has been lost, is perceived as the domain of the medical profession alone. Again, the power is not ours, but the doctor's. So it is that our most basic beliefs about health make health itself improbable because those beliefs support personal impotence in these matters.

Another factor which contributes to illness is the mere presence of our various medical out-reach programs. The popular notion is that more people are being treated for medical problems than ever before because, at long last, we are reaching those who were previously unable to get help. They are coming out of the closet, so to speak. I dispute this. I think, more often than not, we are being provided with a safe means of expressing vulnerability in terms of physical ailments. We can afford to be sick today in a way we never could before. I would never advocate the denial of this help, but as long as we believe that illness "just happens" we will not be able to address the deeper questions of why so many more people are getting sick. What is it about our society which makes people feel increasingly that they cannot cope? What makes them feel so vulnerable and so hopeless?

Whatever the cause of the tremendous rise in those needing medical attention, it is a fact that we now feel safer and less threatened by sickness and disease because there is usually a doctor nearby and he costs us nothing (in most cases). Staying well is not the practical necessity it was once.

I'm reminded of Flora Thompson's *Larkrise to Candleford,* a delightful account of rural, late nineteenth century England. The author recalls the time the itinerant apothecary came to her village. It wasn't long before the entire population began to evince symptoms which only the apothecary's magic little pills could cure. Soon all conversation in the village turned on a comparison of illnesses and the respective potions which could restore health. This adventure into poor health became the village's biggest and most exciting new challenge. Before many months, however, the apothecary packed up and left as mysteriously as he had come. Without his pills to guarantee eventual health, the town could no longer afford this self-indulgence and it wasn't long before everyone's health was restored as mysteriously as it had disappeared. Given human psychology, that apothecary would never go hungry for he would automatically create a need for his services wherever he went. A sort of Typhoid Murray.

Nor is it any different in the late twentieth century. Some years ago, the hospital physicians of San Francisco went out on strike. It was an event made for the media. They searched with great diligence for someone who was to be denied essential treatment because of the doctors' "disregard for public safety." They found no one. Quite suddenly, no one needed a doctor—a fact which just may have hastened the doctors' return to work!

In addition to not having to stay well because medical help is so readily available, insurance and numerous government programs give us this help "free." (Ha!) Hence, there is also little financial incentive to stay on our feet for a physical mis-adventure will no longer bring us to financial ruin. Additionally, few of us like to pay for something we don't get. Our sense of fair play almost compels us to get something back on our investment. Statistics bear out the fact, for instance, that—in great preponderance—people get sick with diseases and other trauma which are covered by their insurance policies. They do not get sick in areas which are not so covered. And you thought we were not a clever lot!

What's more, there is no stigma attached to illness. On the contrary, we can rely upon the complete sympathy of our friends and the centered attention and concern of our families (no questions asked) when we are physically afflicted. In so many ways, physical disability can instantly gratify some very deep needs to be tended, coddled, even reverenced—needs which we dare not express overtly because we like to be such good soldiers about such tender wants. The physical discomfort of being sick can be a small price to pay for such re-assuring emotional benefits.

*　*　*

It is impossible to run to ground every destructive belief which arises from the improper assumption that maintaining health is beyond personal control. For instance, when we state, "Whenever I have a headache, I always take an aspirin," we automatically absent ourselves from the healing process and give that power to the aspirin. And how many times have we all heard, "Look at all those calories!" when dessert is brought to the table? With a statement like this we remind ourselves that calories create fat. Weight becomes something over which we have no control unless we abstain from "all those calories."

The statement, "If you don't wear your sweater, you are going to catch cold," is a statement of belief. It gives hypnotic suggestion that our environment is dangerous and stronger than we are.

The dictim, "See your doctor if pain persists," is a statement of belief. It gives hypnotic suggestion that only a doctor can be effective "if pain persists."

The assertion, "Of course, I have medical insurance. You never know when you'll have to go to the hospital," is a statement of belief. It gives hypnotic suggestion that health is elusive, accidental, and no one has protection from sudden illness. Such matters are out of our hands.

"My mother has diabetes and there is a good chance that I will have it too" is a statement of belief. It gives hypnotic suggestion that the body is powerless to alter a preprogrammed condition.

"What can you expect but the breakdown of the body when you get older?" is a statement of belief. It gives hypnotic suggestion that getting older is synonomous with failing health.

While I cannot take up the cause of health, belief by belief, I can take examples of some commonly held beliefs and explain why I think these specific beliefs may be destructive. After that, you can decide what to do about your own belief system. The truth is that to the degree that we can trust ourselves and our bodies, to that same degree we can experience health. Health is ours if we want it. The stinger is that we must develop our trust *before* we see the results. That's difficult. We like to have results amply demonstrated before we make a trusting leap to a different belief. Without that leap, however, all we will be able to out-picture is the absence of that faith, or illness. Call the system under which we operate a system of self-fulfilling prophecies, remembering that as you believe, so shall it appear.

*   *   *

We believe that the recovery from any illness is accounted for because of something the doctor did or because of the medication or therapy he prescribed. The fact is that no doctor, no medicine, no therapy can cure even the tiniest scratch. It is the body's own miraculous healing power which does it all. By following the doctor's advice the body may be assisted in the healing process, but every speck of health you possess is direct proof of the body's great recuperative powers.

Think for a moment. If the body has the capacity to create disease, it also has the capacity to create health. *If we let it.* If it can perform magic on one side of the ledger, it can perform magic on the other. *If we let it.* We witness this very same magic with every breath and yet we oppose such witnessed fact with imagined fears. Actually creating health is easier for the body because it is more natural. The true astonishment is that the body is so willing to obey our destructive orders which force it to out-picture illness. When it obeys those orders, it diminishes its inherent possibilities and demonstrates, instead, an *alien* ineffectiveness. The next time something goes wrong with your body, acknowledge that what the body has done, it can undo with even greater ease. This statement alone will help enormously in getting rid of unwanted symptoms.

No doctor and no medication can even assist in the process of healing unless the body (and that really means you) permits this help. Another way of saying this is that God cures and the doctor collects the fee. The principle cause of any doctor's success is our own belief that he can, indeed, help. We switch from believing in our illness to believing in our recovery—a recovery we then attribute to something the doctor may have done.

Psychic (faith) healers receive their "miraculous" powers from the identical source—the patient's belief that the healer can effect miracles. The healer's task is to convince those who would be healed that a cure is possible. Belief systems which support the notion that Jesus was and is still an omnipotent healer can provide this kind of confidence for the believer. So also can a string of degrees, licenses, and the title *doctor* provide the same kind of confidence. A believer (of any persuasion) then thinks health is possible because of this new alliance with an efficacious savior. The optimism this inspires releases the patient (and therefore his body) from the bonds imposed by self-assigned impotence. A cure can then be effected because the body's own resources have been fully engaged to fulfill that faith. Healer and doctor alike are being credited with something *we* do for ourselves! The trouble is we don't credit ourselves. We credit the doctor or the healer and therefore continue to believe that they are powerful and we are not. This is wrong. We are powerful and they can only assist us to get in touch with that power.

For this reason, I prefer not to heal psychically though it is easy enough to do. In order to bypass the patient's own imagined inadequacies, I must convince him that I have a power he himself does not possess. I feel this to be dishonest and, in the long run, destructive. Instead, I bend my efforts to building my patient's self-confidence. I prefer that they know that they can produce their own miracles. This is real cause for celebration.

*   *   *

The out-pictured symptoms of disease and illness are caused by feelings of impotence and inadequacy in the first place. In such a threatening emotional state, we need every ounce of self-confidence we can summon if we are going to recover health. Yet most doctors demand (and we eagerly agree) that we place ourselves, like so many damp Kleenexes, under *their* control. While allowing an "expert" to take over can allay destructive fears, it is not a good choice. Did you know that those who do *not* see a doctor regularly stay healthier? That those who do *not* follow his advice get better faster? Those who conducted the survey properly concluded that people who take charge of their own health manage that health better.

Given the fear and discomfort which illness can create, going limp on the doctor's doorstep is probably natural, but what makes me mad is that doctors do everything they can to encourage this posture and hospitals demand it. I recognize that if you are overwhelmed by fear and pain, it is hardly the time to initiate a pitched battle over your rights to dignity, respect, and involvement in the healing process. On the other hand, the more you entitle yourself, the sooner you will recover. This is why those who do not heed the doctor's advice get better sooner.

Unfortunately, it is increasingly the opinion of the government, the courts, and the medical community itself that a medical advisor's opinion should carry with it the force of law. Therapy is forced upon unwilling patients, parents are prosecuted for decisions they make if those decisions run counter to what the medical profession currently favors. How many women remember being told only a few short years ago that in order to eradicate breast cancer they *had* to have most of their chest and back tissue removed? Fads are as prevalent in medicine as anywhere else, yet because too many doctors believe in their own omniscience, these fads can now be forced upon us—legally. I can think of no other expert with an opinion for hire who is able to force his advice upon his client.

Does it help to see your doctor more as an advisor and less as a God to tell you that, in California, the Public Health Department had determined that at least 10% of the state's physicians are so functionally impaired that they should not conduct their business without supervision? Their problems, so says the report, are alcohol, drugs, and general incompetence.

I once listened to my dear aunt and uncle argue about when my uncle would be able to lift more than a few pounds. Home from the hospital following an operation, his doctor had told him not to lift anything for 10 days. Was the prescribed 10 days to commence with his entry into the hospital or his departure from it? You many think this a reasonable argument for the non-professional peasantry, although it is a decision I would maintain is clearly best known by the patient. But my uncle, though now retired, had been a doctor for 50 years! He had been giving that kind of order with all the assumed authority of his profession for most of his life. But suddenly he was playing the role of the ignorant patient. He was so convinced that the doctor knew and the patient didn't know that when he became a patient, obligingly, he no longer knew. We do this with doctors and it is not in our self-interest. If you consult a doctor, you should consult him as an advisor, not as an omnipotent savior. Underneath it all, he knows he isn't and the expectations we place upon him (and he assumes) could drive anyone to drink or drugs or general incompetence.

*   *   *

Everything about a hospital is designed to fill the needs of its personnel. Patient needs which get in the way of the staff are overridden. From the ignoble little johnny coat to the rules which permit a patient to leave only at a time convenient to the accounting department, hospitals insidiously strip their patients of self-respect and autonomy—the very psychological conditions necessary for effective healing. In addition, hospitalization requires that the patient simultaneously abandon all his support systems—his family, his familiar foods, his usual habits, his reassuring surroundings. I call such disregard for the patient's needs sadistic. It is a testament, I believe, to the body's miraculous healing powers that anyone survives hospital treatment.

Because most of us have hospital insurance, we are tied to whatever hospital services are available because they are "free." On the other hand, if you think you may require hospital services in the future, I urge you to consider alternatives *before* the ambulance comes and they trundle you off on a guerney. At that point you will be too indifferent to what is happening to take effective control. Our treatment of the sick is almost as counter-productive as our treatment of criminals, and hospitals, as they are presently organized, should be eliminated in the name of health.

A healing environment should include lots of fresh air, sunshine, plant life and earth. Moving water and animal life can also assist the healing process. These elements offer much more than a psychological feeling of comfort. They directly support the healing process with good and positive energy. Yet hospitals, as a matter of policy, exclude these free cures.

Again, if you look forward to a serious illness, plan to keep as many of your support systems as possible. Keep your family close. (In China, the family moves right in with the patient, tending and feeding him with its own home cooking.) Keep your cocktails, your morning paper, even your own bed if you can. In other words, try to stay home.

Humor is another concomitant of an optimum healing environment. All learning and all healing is markedly progressed by laughter. Laughter automatically puts us in a mental state of good health and receptivity. We cannot laugh when we feel oppressed but we can laugh when we feel effective—and feeling effective is what healing is all about.

*   *   *

We believe we get sick because we "catch" something, like a germ or a virus. The message this belief gives the body is that it lives in an environment it should fear. We tell our bodies that they have little or no power to combat their very surroundings. Yet the ignored truth is that all of us—the sickly and the healthy alike—are subjected, by and large, to the same environment. How come some get sick and some don't? How come doctors and nurses, who are constantly around germs, don't constantly catch something?

Fears about germs arise in part because medical science doesn't study the healthy to find out why and how they maintain health. Instead, it absorbs itself with disease. Because it knows little about health, what it studies frightens it. In turn, doctors convey their fears to us. Thus directed, we pick and choose our facts about health and disease in obedience to our fears. We ignore the marvel of the child who doesn't get chicken pox two weeks after Jimmy's birthday party and note instead the child who does.

Health is a by-product of a state of mind. Some might call that state of mind spiritual attunement. Some of us are more attuned than others; they are the healthy ones. If you wish health, you must first achieve a degree of attunement. Then germs will not find an inviting home in you, for germs are but the available agents you use to express inner *dis*-ease.

The subject of environment brings up air pollution, acid rain, Love Canal, and other chemical plagues we confront in the late twentieth century. It also brings up spiritual attunement again. The laws of nature are founded on the me-AND-you principle. This principle holds that the needs of all must be balanced. As we believe we must conquer nature or be its victim, we operate from a me-OR-you (survival) point of view as far as the earth itself is concerned. At the economic level, the me-OR-you point of view endorses financial greed. On a human level, this same point of view supports the notion that might makes right. Therefore three very important areas of our lives converge to sanction the use of toxic chemicals with little restraint or responsibility. Nature's sign says, GO BACK, WRONG WAY. Nature means what she says. Those who have been victimized by such cultural attitudes (Love Canal residents, for instance) have, for their own unconscious purposes chosen to write their personal scripts in such a way that society as a whole can, if it wishes, understand its own folly.

*   *   *

We live in an adolescent culture which equates rambunctious sexual appetite with power. While the adoration we bestow upon our youth may compensate them, in some measure, for their lack of wisdom and experience, it offers no one, particularly the young, any reason to rejoice in what lies ahead. Yet anticipation is the very soul of life and each phase of life has its own rich opportunities and rewards. Speaking for myself, each new decade is much richer than the one which preceded it because I choose to make it that way. I have more freedom, I am wiser, I know my likes and dislikes better, I am more appreciative. The list goes on.

As a culture, we believe that old age is synonymous with poor health. There is absolutely no need to stumble into our twilight years in a torment of failing health. Such conditions result from our expectations that this is "natural." Discarding a body (dying) need be no different than discarding a suit of clothing. There is no inherent mandate that we tear either to shreds before we are done with them. We can all die like my friend Ann if we wish. She moved from a full day of vigorous activity to a death so quiet and painless that her son, who was watching television with her, did not know when she died.

There is a little town in England which is notable because so many of its folk live *active* lives well beyond their hundredth year. When asked the reasons for this longevity, they cannot explain it. "It's just what we expect will happen," they apologize, as if by giving the true explanation they are offering no explanation at all.

I rather suspect that Methuselah did, indeed, live 969 years. But he probably earned his reputation for longevity, not because he lived 13 of our lifetimes, but because his contemporaries only made it to 800 years or so. Because we do not believe in health, such a long life would constitute a terrible punishment from which we are mercifully spared. On the other hand, if we did believe in health, we could spend the richest years of our lives having fun. It is a matter of choice, not accident, if this occurs.

*   *   *

We believe we are what we eat. Most of us have either made mealtime a ritual in self-denial or a drug program, depending upon our persuasions. Because we imagine that the body needs all the help it can get and that the very act of eating can damage the body or help it, few of us escape the current mania of evaluating all food in terms of its laboratory analysis. If Breatharians (those are the people who claim to eat *nothing*) can manage, doesn't this tell us that food may have only a supplemental value? That sun, water, and air may supply all we *must* have? How much of a particular food's value, then, may lie with the joy of eating it rather than the chemical make-up of that food? Edgar Cayce, the transmedium whose ability to get in touch with any piece of information has generated a shelf of books, said that food would do for you what you thought it would do for you. Restated in my own words, he said that foods are talismans to which we attribute power, not inherently theirs.

If you believe that only a "correct" diet can insure health there is probably very little I can say to dissuade you from making your meals into chemical therapy sessions. I can, however, point out that today's favored food is likely to be tomorrow's anathema. Tomatoes, for instance, were once thought to be poisonous and milk is currently under suspicion. But for those of you who would like to relax your shoulds and shouldn'ts a bit, let me at least present a point of view at variance with commonly accepted beliefs about food. It might start an examination of some of your current beliefs.

The secret of the body's successful use of foodstuffs is transmutation. It takes what is available and makes out of that what it needs. We don't see it that way. We believe we must supply the body directly with what it needs—so much vitamin B, so much protein, etc.—as if it could only deal with the ready-made garment and had no tailoring abilities of its own.

Let's use protein as an example. Muscles, we are told, are made from protein. So depending upon our size, we must consume x grams of complete protein in order to maintain our musculature. But what of the cow? How come she survives so well on grass which offers almost no complete protein? The claim is that herbivorous stomachs are different from those of omnivores. Is that really true or has a *psychological* preference made hay less beneficial? How much does the *feeling* of being well fed after a beef dinner affect the nourishment value of the meat? How much complete protein do vegetarians get if they don't use milk products? Are they as healthy as the rest of the population? If so, why? If not, do they perhaps see their diet as a program of self-denial? In other words, if we were conditioned emotionally to live on grains alone, would we manage as well? My own intuition tells me than any diet which feeds the soul in all its subjective preferences, feeds the body perfectly.

It is said that the body does not manufacture vitamins and that we must obtain these essentials from the food we eat. Scurvy, a so-called vitamin C deficiency disease, was first treated by the British Navy by introducing limes into the diets of its sailors. But I wonder about vitamin C. It does not seem logical to me that the body cannot produce its own vitamin C, or at least its own version of vitamin C's beneficial properties. For instance, what about the diet of old-time Eskimos? Where does their vitamin C come from? Liver contains a small amount of vitamin C, of course, but enough to off-set the absence of all fruits and vegetables? Besides, you would have to eat an awful lot of polar bear to get a little liver, so the amount is even further diluted.

Let's go back to those sailors. I wonder if the sailors' scurvy hadn't more to do with homesickness than with vitamin C. The vitamin is primarily a detoxifying agent. To me the elevation of toxic agents in the body and the subsequent "deficiency" symptoms suggests "poisonous" feelings, disgruntlement perhaps. Could sex, for instance, have been even more efficacious than limes? I'm not suggesting that limes do not cure the symptoms of scurvy or are not a positive additive once the system has been rendered toxic for psychological reasons. But I am implying that a vitamin C deficiency is caused for reasons other than its presumed absence from the diet. I am also implying that mental contentment will enable our bodies to produce internally whatever is needed to reflect that contentment. And the physical out-picturing of mental contentment is health.

*   *   *

Currently, one of our most popular fears is cholesterol. The body manufactures both cholesterol and the substance which controls cholesterol, lecithin. Both cholesterol and lecithin are absolutely indispensable to the proper functioning of the body. High blood cholesterol suggests that the body lacks lecithin. Yet eggs, banned by low cholesterol devotees, are rich in lecithin. You would think, believing as we do in fighting a symptom with a counter symptom[1] that we would be dosing ourselves with lecithin except that I suspect we rather enjoy self-deprival. High cholesterol foods are usually such fun to eat.

In all events, low cholesterol diets cause the liver to *increase* its own production of cholesterol. High cholesterol diets *decrease* the liver's production as the body tries to create what it needs from

[1]Allopathic medicine, to which we are *legally* committed through the efforts of the American Medical Association, is "the method of treating disease by the use of agents producing effects different than those treated." (Not very reassuring, is it?) *Grolier Webster International Dictionary*, 1976.

what it is given. The ratio between cholesterol and lecithin is demonstrably determined by something other than diet. Thus, to manipulate it by diet may only compound the problem. Cholesterol starvation, for instance, can produce heart disease. This means that while we are supposedly clearing up our atherosclerosis with a low cholesterol diet we may be inviting congestive heart failure! That's not much of a solution to a health problem is it?

Tinkering with an organic equation is not simplistic. The effects go off in all directions. Additionally, if the body is forced to abnormal habits of production, the body may begin to accept abnormal as normal. In this respect, both food and drugs can have the same effect upon the body. They can produce dependency.

Edgar Cayce has this to say about additives such as vitamins: "All such properties that add to the system are more efficacious if they are given for periods, left off for periods and begun again. For if the system comes to rely upon such influences wholly, *it ceases to produce the vitamins* (emphasis added) even though the food values may be normally balanced. And it is better that *these be produced in the body in the normal development* (emphasis added) than supplied mechanically, for nature is much better yet than science!"[2]

There are some very rich doctors who confine their practices exclusively to treating the drug disorders other doctors create. *All drugs have side effects.* Even the innocent little aspirin causes the stomach to bleed up to a teaspoon of blood per pill. Some of those "side effects" include death. Penicillin, for instance, can produce irreversible anaphylactic shock.

In addition to the direct side effects, however, there may be long term effects which we are not even considering. In the 60's, gonorrhea began to reach epidemic proportions. In part this may have been due to a social change in sexual mores and the increase

---

[2]Direct quote from the readings reproduced by Dr. Harold J. Reilly's book, *The Edgar Cayce Handbook for Health Through Drugless Therapy.* Macmillan Publishing Co., New York, 1975, pg. 79.

in casual sex. But that generation was also the first generation to receive antibiotics from birth for every sniffle and sneeze. I suspect that bodies which are not required to manufacture their own antibiotics believe that this non-production is "normal" and therefore no longer maintain optimum production. Such bodies may even be unable to produce antibiotics (Acquired Immune Deficiency Syndrome?). Put succinctly, the forced introduction of antibiotics as a drug may have impaired or even killed the golden goose which keeps our immune systems functioning properly. Perhaps that innocent little aspirin (about which we know very little in spite of its widespread use) may be closing down the production of endorphines, a natural pain killer produced by the body. It is a point to consider the next time you blithely decide to pop a pill or eat a contrived diet.

I'm convinced that we embrace a health-through-chemistry approach to well-being because it sounds simple and it appears reasonable, given a scientific model of the body which is itself simplistic in that it ignores overriding cause. In the case of cholesterol/lecithin that cause is what determines the ratio between the two substances and jiggering with the simple equation between them doesn't address this at all. Health is ecological in nature. It is derived from subtle relationships which must be considered as a whole and in a complete context. The cause of health lies within beliefs about life and about the body. You can control health from that level and guarantee the correct chemical balances automatically, and without side-effects, as nature intended.

* * *

One of the great lines to come out of the Mary Tyler Moore Show was, "Do you remember the days before there were any calories?" In a laboratory, a calorie may be a heat unit, but to 90% of the population, calories are what we eat. Calories have replaced food. Yet calories, *per se*, do not create fat. The creation of fat is basically a metabolic matter. The metabolic system has not been set at a pace equal to our intake. But here again, cause lies in the management of that system, not in the calories themselves. All of us know veritable bean poles who eat enough for three and we all have fat friends who eat with relative modesty. The proper use of what the body is given is determined by the mind. So is the appetite.

If I am a judge, the French eat twice as much as the Americans yet they don't have a national weight problem. But then, they truly enjoy food and are not likely to make an enemy of such a friend. Americans, on the other hand, seem to dread almost everything they put into their mouths unless it is a pill. Americans have given the calorie a power which only fear can bestow and only faith in the self can deny.

Do you remember that I said that the way to create a war was to advocate it, to fear it, or to oppose it? The way to create fat is to work against it. If you want to be thin, strongly imagine yourself as a thin person. You must never do battle with your fat, else you will be creating it even as you starve yourself.

If you must make the pleasure of eating into a health ritual, may I suggest fresh foods, locally and naturally grown, and lovingly prepared. An affirmation expressing your confidence in your body's ability to create health wouldn't hurt either.

Health is a matter of releasing ourselves from our beliefs in illness, from our belief in the inability of the body to take care of itself, and from our beliefs in our own impotence to control properly the body's functions. We are in charge at all times whether we acknowledge it or not. The body is completely dedicated to its own good health but it must function according to the commands given to it. Illness, therefore, is self-inflicted. We will find cause for why we inflict illness upon ourselves in our belief systems.

16.

Interpreting Physical Symptoms

ALL EVENTS ARE PRODUCED by the endospheric mind as it describes its own emotional state and the beliefs through which it defines itself. Unpleasant physical symptoms are the symbolic out-picturings of emotional/mental distress. If we read those symbols correctly we can pinpoint the specific belief which is causing the unwanted symptom to appear and make specific adjustments in the belief system which is creating the harm. The symptom will then disappear and we will speed our recovery. If we do a thorough job of eradicating cause, many future illnesses can be avoided.

All untoward events in our lives demonstrate that we are off-track "spiritually." Our thinking is not compatible with the truth, the truth that we are strong and effective as individuals and have nothing to fear. Any belief which supports a contrary position may be the belief which is manifesting negatively at the moment. The question is: Which, among so many beliefs, is the one which needs to be changed? Learning to interpret the symbolic speech of the body can be of enormous help in such a quest, particularly as the body always tells the truth. We, you see, are being troubled with what we have chosen *not* to acknowledge. Had we acknowledged these feelings, the body would have no need for such covert expression. But this also means—unfortunately—that our intellectual assessment of what *is* truly important to us is almost useless. Reading the body's symptoms therefore can be like referring back to the minutes of a meeting we hardly realized we had attended.

When it comes to interpreting what our physical symptoms symbolize in terms of negative beliefs, our job is made much simpler than with circumstantial events. All bodies are pretty much the same. Moreover, the body is run from energy centers called chakrahs (shock-rahs) which have very specific responsibilities. Knowing of these physical and mental responsibilities makes it far easier to pinpoint the mental cause of physical effect because each chakrah has already made this connection for us. It is therefore of considerable benefit to our quest for cause to know something of chakrahs and their areas of expertise.

Before we get to our discussion of chakrahs, let me point out that much of what I will have to say about which chakrah influences what organ or system, comes principally from my personal intuition and logic, but little more. Such a scheme as I indicate is a crude beginning in an unexplored field. It therefore should be taken as suggestive only. Additionally, the body always functions as a unified whole and my rather arbitrary separations oversimplify in all cases.

I also wish to be brief. I therefore suffer from a disquietude that the correlations of a symptom to its root cause too often sound like what I call Dream Book Wisdom. You know the kind of pulp paper advice I'm talking about. "Dream of a dove and you will get a letter from a loved one." "Dream of a balloon and this means that you have not got your feet on the ground." To my mind such correlations are so much garbage. They are simplistic to the point of fraud, for we are all individuals with individual ways of expressing ourselves. Be guided, then, by my suggestions but do not consider them inviolate. It is you who write your script, not I.

To a psychic, a chakrah looks like a luminous spot about the size of a quarter. There are seven principle chakrahs running in a connected energy line from the base of the spine to the top of the head. This line is transected by another line which crosses the upper chest and terminates in the palms of the hands. Lines of energy also run from the first chakrah at the base of the spine down the legs to the insteps. These chakrahs are the only ones we will be discussing although there are minor ones throughout the body.

Chakrahs spin in four directions simultaneously—inward, outward, clockwise, and counter-clockwise. Chakrahs not only provide the energy which supports life itself, but they direct the body and its functions. Incidentally, chakrahs are not a new discovery. Knowledge of them extends back into antiquity.

Each chakrah sends, receives, and stores information relevant to its own particular area of responsibility. Chakrahs dilate or contract at will, much like the pupil of the eye. Usually, however, we find a comfortable way of managing this energy and the chakrahs tend, therefore, to stabilize into a personal and characteristic pattern. That is, we will choose (or need) to keep some chakrahs wide open while we will choose to close others down. These decisions not only can distort the flow of energy but they can also affect our sensitivity to particular kinds of occurrences around us.

For instance, if the fourth, or heart, chakrah is overly dilated, we may find ourselves falling in love too easily. Conversely, if the heart chakrah is shut down too tightly, we may be presenting ourselves as too uncaring. All of this, of course, is in addition to what an improper flow of psychic energy does to the physical heart directly. Dilation floods it with energy with which it is not equipped to deal. Constriction starves it of energy it must have to maintain its health.

Beliefs directly affect chakrahs. Chakrahs, in turn, directly affect the body. It is possible to make some very therapeutic changes in our lives by attacking a problem directly at the chakrah level. I once read a young woman whose chakrahs were *all* dilated. This is

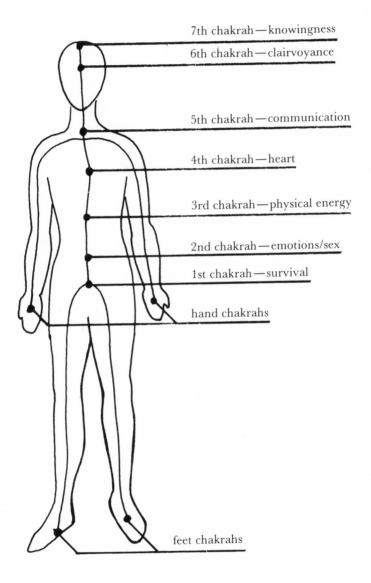

Fig. 1. Chakrahs

most unusual. She couldn't stop talking or end a sentence once she began it. Nor could she sit still in her "hyper" fright. By concentrating her attention on her chakrahs and stipulating that they be closed down, she was able to clamp down sufficiently so that she was no longer in such distress. You can also stipulate that these centers be clean. This will affect any negativity which might be involved in the improper functioning of the chakrah. Such chakrah meditation is a halfway measure, but it is a very positive halfway measure.

In addition to running the body, chakrahs gather information in the service of that function. In a state of stress or emergency, the relevant chakrah or chakrahs will dilate, the better to read the nuances of a given situation. However, if it remains dilated after the specific experience is over, perhaps because unresolved anxiety related to the experience is forcing it to stay open, the chakrah can pick up too much information and cause the body to stay "battle-ready." In a sense, the chakrah becomes paranoiac and it sends out its orders to the body on the basis of this paranoia. There is a sensory and energy overload coming to and from this chakrah. This can lead to unreasonable emotional anxiety as well as serious physical disorders.

Because chakrahs also send out information to others on a psychic level, we sometimes wish to intercept this natural communication with others by closing down a particular chakrah. We "hide." When we do this we not only block subliminal communication, but we can starve the body of its needed psychic energy.

Chakrahs are much more informative and fascinating than our present discussion can indicate. I write for the layman who believes he cannot see them. For instance, chakrahs present themselves in color; they spin at a particular but changeable frequency. This means they can be read in terms of their emotional, intellectual, etc., qualities. They also store active (stuck) pictures and sometimes universal symbols like a cross or a pyramid. They spin smoothly or in fits and starts. They are, to a psychic, a veritable dossier on everything which is affecting the self—how well the body is functioning, what memories are still energized, how the personality chooses to present itself, etc.

In Fig. 1, I have given the traditional designation of the specific purpose of each chakrah—knowledge, clairvoyance, etc. Because physical trauma expresses psychological vulnerability, for the purposes of relating the chakrahs to negative beliefs (or fear), I have appointed a specific kind of fear to each chakrah. This, alas, is also the sort of oversimplification which I call Dream Book Wisdom. While I find the system works and works well, I give them to you only as guides. You must judge for yourself how your body is expressing YOU.

Here, then, is a list for your ready referral.

1st chakrah   —   Survival. Fear for physical safety. Fear of physical independence.

2nd chakrah   —   Emotions/sex. Fear for emotional safety. Fear of sexual inadequacy.

3rd chakrah   —   Energy. Fear of personal inadequacy.

4th chakrah   —   Heart. Fear of betrayal and matters of trust.

5th chakrah   —   Communication. Fear of self-expression.

6th chakrah   —   Clairvoyance. Fear of letting go a bias, of being wrong. (This is the "objective" chakrah.)

7th chakrah   —   Knowingness. Fear of autonomy.

*   *   *

The first chakrah is located low in the groin. It is commonly called the survival chakrah and is said to contain all the information on how to survive in a body. For humans—animals have chakrahs, too—the meaning of survival seems to extend itself to include a psychological dependence at the physical level. Do we feel comfortable about looking after our physical needs or do we feel we need to be looked after?

I suspect that the spine, and hence the central nervous system, is controlled from this chakrah. That is to say, it is from this chakrah that appropriate messages are sent out to the brain, and the brain then directs the central nervous system, according to the messages it receives from the first chakrah.

All babies and children are corded—bonded by a "rope" of energy— from their survival chakrahs to their mother's survival chakrahs. The cord is a recognition of the child's physical dependency on the mother and the mother's willingness to take responsibility for that child. It allows the mother to know what is happening to the child and it gives the youngster a feeling of confidence as the child can tap into the mother's survival information. Such arrangements are not only appropriate but necessary for the child.

I have a feeling but do not know, that autism may be one result of denying this cord between parent and child—denied by either the mother or the baby or both—for a disruption at this level can be very serious indeed. Foundling babies who are unable to cord (or bond) in this usual way and can find no surrogate mother who will make this connection of life with them, will die.

At the opposite end, I have also seen couples corded on this level. This is not in the best interests of either the dependent or supporting personality. They are arrangements of extreme need and based on a Stuck Picture which has not allowed proper maturation. It is also a terrible drain on the surrogate parent and it makes adult love impossible.

If dependency is a psychological factor, these feelings can manifest as lower back pain. Let me give you an example of what I mean. Some years ago, I found myself washing and waxing the car. I say *found myself* because it was one of a series of tasks I had been undertaking which, in retrospect, did not seem "natural," both because of the kind of chores they were and my seeming need to be suddenly doing them. If you will forgive my sex bias, they were typically masculine jobs. I was trying to chop wood, working on the roof, and now, for the first time in my life, I was tackling the car, something I had always managed to palm off on a husband or a son.

Again in retrospect, I remembered feeling lonely, abandoned as I went about washing the car. But the feeling was slight—almost a mood cloud which momentarily dimmed my spirits before it moved on. I would have thought no more about it if I hadn't awakened the next morning with a crippling pain in my lower back.

Lying, helpless as a baby (!), I began the sorting-out process which is almost second nature now. I recalled that fleeting mood I had felt as I washed the car. The mood recalled my father who had died some months before. His death had been both timely and dignified and I had not been overly upset. On the other hand, I had just returned from a delayed memorial service for both him and my stepmother. My brother and I had spent some days together, dismantling their home with its mementoes of our entire lifetimes. Yes, I did feel orphaned. But, after all, I was a big girl now. Big girls should expect aging parents to die, shouldn't they?

Yet, somewhere within me, a little girl was feeling bereft. She no longer had her Daddy to take care of her. She would have to take responsibility for herself now. Because I hadn't acknowledged my feelings of dependency and vulnerability, they had to manifest covertly in a reflection of exactly what I was feeling. So there, in the area of my first chakrah, the physical dependency chakrah, was my wish to be dependent ("crippled") and the pain of having no one to take care of me.

After I had traced my condition to its emotional source, I allowed the little girl in me to feel the pain and the fear of having the props pulled out from under her. But I also assured her that everything was going to be fine because there was also a big girl, competent and able in her own right (even to the point of fixing the roof and waxing the car!) who could manage very well without her father. (I didn't mention chopping wood to the little girl. The big girl has not yet mastered the axe!) The pain was almost gone the next morning and it has never bothered me again.

I know many women with lower back pain whose children have left home. Is their sense of dependency linked to their children? Have their children made them feel safe in their roles as mother? Or has their age and their lack of training for today's work force made them more keenly aware of their vulnerable dependence upon their husbands? How many men still sequester "little boy" fears of leaving home and making it on their own, in spite of the fact that the adult may be running a multi-million dollar business? Conversely, are there those who develop lower back pain because they unconsciously wish to cripple themselves in order to give assurances to a parent, a spouse, or even a child, that they remain as loyally dependent as ever? Do they perhaps fear their own acts of independence and what it might do to the relationship?

And what of nervous disorders like Parkinson's Disease? Are these the expressions of someone caught in a trap which makes him dependent? A trap he cannot live with (as an adult) and cannot let go (as a child)? Does the body, caught in this bind, despair and become crippled?

I think of the first (survival) chakrah as being intimately connected with a general fear threshold. In an adult, and under normal conditions, it should be closed down, yet it seldom is. Taking care of oneself should be "second nature" for an adult. If you are the "nervous type," meditatively suggest that this chakrah be closed down. Then ask yourself why you think you cannot make it on your own. If you have some problems with your spine, it may be that you are not "standing up for yourself," or you may be slumped in despair over your imagined inability to care for yourself without help.

*   *   *

The second chakrah is located a few inches below the navel and back towards the spine. It is described as the emotional/sexual chakrah. When this chakrah is open it a great "reader." It is the chakrah we use to sense or "read" the emotional climate around us. Many of us do not feel particularly safe with others. We need to gauge all the emotional nuances being expressed by them and we do this by opening up this chakrah. We are on the lookout for signs of trouble. And trouble we are apt to find. But all too often it isn't ours. On this level of awareness, there is no distinction between the self and others because the endospheric mind makes no distinction between what is real and what is imagined. Pain is pain to this chakrah and it sends out alarms accordingly, no matter from where the actual pain is originating.

In psychic parlance, this is called living off other people's dirty pictures because these pictures are flecked with black or swathed in grey film. If you wish to help others, close down this chakrah when you do so, and you won't be overcome by pain which is not yours. You cannot help a drowning man if you are drowning yourself. You must get yourself to high ground and stop passing gloomy pictures back and forth. Misery may love company but descending into the pit together leaves no one above with a rope.

Often we close down this chakrah in an effort to control anger. Anger can be a very useful self-help tool. Occasionally we need anger for making our needs known and for protecting our space. If we close down the emotional chakrah under these conditions, the self is likely to feel defenseless. Closing down the emotional chakrah out of fear forces the survival chakrah to be inappropriately open. The entire body must then live in a "state of survival" and battle readiness.

My intuition tells me that the second chakrah helps keep the body cleansed of wastes (call those wastes emotional effluvia) and therefore it is the master chakrah for the liver, spleen, kidneys, bladder, bowels, as well as the lymphatic and immune systems. Edema (a form of waste) would be another generalized symptom regulated by this chakrah. Add to all this, the control of the sexual organs as well as a vested interest in the vascular system and you can begin to see how important this chakrah is.

Some ancient chakrah diagrams locate the second chakrah near the liver and others refer to it as the spleen chakrah. The spleen was once thought to be the seat of the emotions, though we now relate its activities to the service of the blood and the lymphatic system. Interestingly, we speak of red blooded he-men and yellow livered cowards—two descriptions of emotional attitudes. One infers the optimum functioning of the spleen and the other a disease of the liver. Turning pale and blushing are also emotional reactions and are produced by changes in the vascular system. And what of the relationship between high blood pressure and suppressed anger? Between low blood pressure and listlessness? I would look to the malfunction of the second chakrah for causes of atherosclerosis, equating, in this instance, excess cholesterol with emotional clogging or Stuck Pictures.

Because I don't think we are able to be deeply happy and sick at the same time, and because negative emotions produce their own kind of wastes, I think the immune system also belongs under the domain of this chakrah. Emotional distress leaves us vulnerable. Or rather, because we feel vulnerable, we experience emotional distress. The body reacts obligingly to those feelings by reflecting this vulnerable condition and lowers its defenses (the immune system). Were I, for instance, investigating AIDS (Acquired Immune Deficiency Syndrome) I would look at the emotional vulnerability level of my patients, believing that despair was playing an important role in the body's inability to defend itself. If those patients were homosexual (and even if they weren't) I would also be interested in whether those who contracted the disease were caught up in playing the "female" or subordinate (vulnerable) role in their partnerships and whether the suppression of "male" character traits was precipitating such vulnerability. In addition, I would ask questions about how the homosexual patient perceived himself in a society which scorns homosexuality. Does his relationship to society induce feelings of vulnerability?

Science has discovered substances called endorphines which are believed to be secreted by the brain to counteract pain. Pain in the body is a reflection of emotional pain. My assumption is that the second chakrah regulates the release of endorphines, depending upon what is required to express outwardly the internal emotional situation. If you are experiencing bodily pain, find the *emotional pain* which is forcing this expression and bring it out into the open. You can also effectively self-hypnotize yourself to feel no pain, another method for getting endorphines into the system.

The second chakrah is also the sexual chakrah. Because we equate sexuality with potency, the emotional self-confidence scale translates itself into the sexual adequacy scale, with vulnerability and sexual impotence at one end and confidence and sexual potency at the other.

As I write this, a man believed to be responsible for a series of trailside killings has been apprehended. With one exception, the victims were all women and that exception was a man accompanying a woman victim. The murder suspect has a second chakrah which, literally, no longer functions. It has no boundaries. (How do I know? I peeked psychically—one of the advantages of seeing on a level which has no space and time.) The place where the chakrah should be has "hemorrhaged" to an area about the size of small phonograph record. His loss of *all control* (for that is what the second chakrah suggests) over his emotional/sexual feelings has two immediately obvious consequences. First, he feels impotent, and second, he would have to be "yelled at" to experience any emotional reaction. That is, he would be unable to experience any emotion within what we consider a normal range. He has become insensitive but his insensitivity was originally created by an over-sensitivity which caused him too much pain. Perhaps an excess of other people's dirty pictures?

(The trial of this man is now over. Before the summation, his lawyer pleaded him guilty. Courtroom witnesses were particularly struck by the man's total lack of all emotion throughout a rather grizzly trial.)

The man is not insane, however. He has a vibrant aura from the fourth chakrah on up, where his head is. There is also a large piece missing on the level of this fifth chakrah. This is the communication center. It suggests some serious speech problems. (I know now he has a bad stutter.) From the bottom of his sternum downward there is nothing but a thick black veil. This suggests terrible pain and distress. His problems are second chakrah problems; they are emotional and sexual problems.

*   *   *

The third chakrah is above the navel in the solar plexus. It is the body's energy center. I think of this chakrah as expressing the purpose of will or self-determination, self-reliance, etc. I associate the third chakrah with the body's metabolic and gastro-intestinal tract. Mood drugs and alcohol drastically affect this chakrah's ability to function properly. When it is overly dilated—as with all chakrahs we have discussed—we are fearful, but the fear expressed in the third chakrah is, I believe, a fear of losing control in a given situation. Paranoia is the extreme psychological example of this feeling but cancer is also rooted in such a loss of control and out-pictures as a breakdown in the body's ability to "control" the malfunctioning of cells.

It may well be that alcohol, drugs, etc., release the third chakrah from self-imposed suppression and moves it to dilation or "loss of control," principally because the self thinks suppression is normal. Therefore, anything less restricted would be considered "out of control" by the self. In other words, if we were not so uptight about being "in control" we wouldn't have to relax with drugs. Is it also possible that those who habitually "lose control" by dilating this chakrah excessively through alcohol and drugs are laying the groundwork for cancer?

Characteristically, most people have the first and third chakrahs too open and the second chakrah too closed. This means that their fears of independence are related to their fears of personal inadequacy. And this is why oversimplification is not always helpful. The system runs as an integrated whole. In addition, some of the pressure to dilate the first and third chakrahs is coming from an improper management of the second chakrah, hampered as it is by the belief that emotions must be well controlled.

The line of energy running from chakrah to chakrah is best thought of as rubber tube which can be pinched off or distended at the chakrah points. Pinching will constrict the flow of energy. Distending the tubing can weaken the walls and form a pool. The system itself, however, will always attempt to equalize these variations.

Weight problems, dietary problems—including diabetes, hypoglycemia, etc.—suggest that the third chakrah is not functioning properly. I tend to believe that behind these disorders there may be a mother relationship which has not been de-energized. The chakrah is at the approximate site of the intrauterine mother/foetus connection, the umbilical cord. Proper separations between mother and child (of any age) may not have been completed. Is the sufferer of metabolic and gastro-intestinal disorders still mother dependent? Remember that not all parts of us are usually grown up. Are those afflicted, fighting the right/wrong game on the mother/child level, saying, "You don't love me," and then "proving" it by denying the body its proper (mothering) nourishment? It is in this direction that I would look were I investigating the endospheric causes of such diseases.

The third chakrah is involved in the kind of healings I do. In essence, I impose my "healing will" by cording, or bonding, with the patient at this level. This is also the chakrah into which the "vampire" plugs his cord. A vampire, in my language, is a person who unconsciously (usually) drains the energy of another for his own purposes. He's the one who gets more and more animated as you grow increasingly exhausted. Many people drain the energy of others to some extent but there are those who can be very dangerous to those close to them. I have fainted on more than one occasion in the close company of one vampire I knew because my third chakrah was too open. If you are a healer, you must be sure to keep this chakrah closed except when you are actually healing. Many people are healers. Healers tend to think they can save the world, or at least their friends, and they tend to "bleed" their own energy in that cause.

Such nonsense can and should be stopped immediately by making separations mentally between yourself and the vampire. The vampire may think you lack some of your old charm but at least you won't be exhausted. People who think they must always be giving of themselves do so, in part, because they think they have no real value in and of themselves.

The third chakrah permits the astral body to escape the physical body on its way to various adventures. The astral body is secured to the physical body at this chakrah by a silver cord, so called because it is luminous, like all cords, to a psychic. On the astral level there is no such thing as unconsciousness. It is only the body from which consciousness more or less departs in sleep or trauma. Anyone working around an unconscious body should be aware that negative remarks or actions can have a devastating effect on the patient because a very aware consciousness is taking it all in on another level, whether or not the experience is consciously remembered later.

If you have ever been awakened from a half-sleep by a shuddering, it is likely that you have yanked the astral body back because you did not feel yourself to be sufficiently asleep to let it go. Those who experiment consciously with astral travel can be quite frightened when it actually starts to happen and may abruptly change their minds. A true physical emergency can also bring the astral body tumbling back to the physical body. So can a remarkable dream (good or bad). The astral (dreaming) self may want out of a nightmare or may wish the body's conscious attention for some other purpose.

*   *   *

The fourth chakrah is the heart or affinity chakrah. It is located beneath the sternum and a bit to the left. The heart itself is under the fourth chakrah's influence. So, too, is blood circulation. This chakrah attracts grief pictures even more effectively than the second chakrah. It is therefore as likely, from a layman's point of view, that symptoms like high blood cholesterol, faulty blood pressure, etc., are coming from the malfunction of this chakrah as they are from the malfunction of the second chakrah.

The fourth chakrah can become so gummed up with emotional debris that it looks like the moon, caught in a dust pan of tinker toys and dust bunnies. The heart can take a lot of abuse, but heartache, left unresolved, will ultimately damage the heart. All heartache must be de-energized, or neutralized or it will fester around this chakrah and cause it to malfunction.

Fears, on the heart level, address themselves to trust and the betrayal of that trust. We fear being rejected, rebuffed, disappointed, not having our expectations fulfilled, etc. It is small wonder that so many of us die of massive heart problems. Old griefs and old pains may be in the past as far as the self is concerned, but if they are unresolved, they remain in the present in this chakrah as well as others. This causes the chakrah to malfunction in the same way you would expect dirt to damage any machinery. Some people even go so far as to have a piece of this chakrah missing. This is caused by a lie. (See Chapter 11.)

*   *   *

The fifth chakrah is located at the base of the neck. It is the communication chakrah. Its most obvious role concerns speech, but the throat, the mouth, and the ears are also under the domain of this chakrah. In addition, I believe, the fifth chakrah is the master chakrah for the respiratory system—the nose, the lungs, and the general oxidation of the body through the blood stream. I think of it as the giving and receiving chakrah. The lungs, for instance, take in and expel air, as do the nose and the mouth. The mouth takes in food; it can also expel it! The mouth also expresses the mind outwardly and the ears take in communication.

The fifth chakrah is located very near the juncture of a lateral system of energy which runs across the uppermost chest and down each arm to the palms. Hands are, most obviously, physical givers and receivers. They are also energy givers/receivers. They can heal (if the energy is good) and they can read psychically, or receive information.

Perhaps the subliminal cross created by the intersection of these two lines of psychic energy is the prototype for the cross, a nearly ubiquitous spiritual symbol, the use of which predates, by far, its Christian origin. And while we are on the subject of symbols, what of the swastika, the use of which goes back into man's historical dawn? Is it not the swirling chakrah? I think it fair to assume that "primitive" man was far more psychic than we. His spiritual wisdom very probably exceeded our own because we concentrate so heavily on the physical look of things. We look at the effect but never at the cause which, by its very nature, is always "invisible."

I would first try to find the cause of any problem under the domain of the fifth chakrah by looking for a perceived imbalance in giving/receiving between the self and others. (This also can mean the perception that you give too little to yourself!) Another way of looking at giving is to call it self-expression. Too often, we may withhold giving because what we truly want to give is a poke in the eye. We want to express the self in hostility. Unwilling to do this, we suppress the action of this chakrah, slink into the role of victim, and send out "I am vulnerable" messages to the body instead of saying what's on our minds. Thus our respiratory system, for instance, will dutifully reflect this vulnerability and lose its ability to deal with bacteria, viruses, and the like. We catch cold.

If you have lung problems—colds, pneumonia, asthma, emphysema, cancer, etc.—it may be your suppressed anger which is causing the congestion. People in an on-going state of anger are angry because, beneath it all, they are afraid they cannot manage. They are angry at others because they prefer to blame others for events they experience rather than search out the fear of inadequacy within themselves. Actually, all of us are very adequate indeed. Only fear blocks our being able to see this. At any rate, all of these kinds of equations between ourselves and others are giving/taking equations. We either believe we are not getting our share or we deny the gifts of others to validate our beliefs that no one cares.

The fifth chakrah, like the second chakrah, is particularly vulnerable to outside influence. There is an associated chakrah at the back of the neck which can be corded—consciously or unconsciously—by carnates and discarnates alike. Such communication may be well intentioned or not, but it can always provide confusion. It is as if we were listening to two or more radio stations simultaneously. If you are not feeling altogether clear in terms of expressing yourself (or, indeed, of understanding what it is you are thinking), stipulate that all cords be broken at the fifth chakrah level and watch your confusion clear up.

Dental and other oral problems probably have much to do with tensions we incur when we repressively monitor what we say and do not say. Perhaps you are being too careful because someone said to you, "You have no right to say that," or "You don't even know what you are talking about." Then, too, there is always the frustration of accurately translating thoughts into words. What self-imposed "I can'ts" are providing a tension which in turn deprives the mouth of its health? What true inner feelings are you not allowing yourself to express outwardly lest they make you less than perfect?

It may also be that the entire endocrine system, the system which produces hormones, is linked to this chakrah, though the usual psychic view is that each gland is associated with the nearest chakrah. I lean towards my own theory because it seems to me that the body may express or *communicate* the physical self through hormones in the same way that speech expresses our inner selves through sound symbols.

*   *   *

The sixth chakrah, located in the center of the lower brow, is commonly called the third eye or the seat of clairvoyance. This chakrah affects vision. Those who are particularly adept at inner visualization, as well as abstract thought (which also must be pictured), are drawing heavily upon the resources of this chakrah. The sixth chakrah is very probably the seat of our sense of humor and our creative originality also.

If you believe you are not psychic, it may be because you have closed down this chakrah. Many people consider such psychic talent frightening, as well as socially unacceptable. But closing down this chakrah can also limit your adventures in creativity as well as affecting physical vision.

The sixth chakrah is also the chakrah which presents us with as much objectivity as we are likely to find in a world founded on subjectivity. By imagining yourself "in" it (or by concentrating your attention upon it) you can escape the pull of the emotions, the ego, and the heart as you sort out a problem. The next time you are putting yourself through the wringer over the dissolution of a love affair or some other failure, get a mental picture of yourself looking at the world through this chakrah and then see what solutions present themselves. I go so far as to imagine a little rocker in the center of my head in which I sit. It's like being a Lilliput in a piece of earth-moving equipment. That image alone can make you feel very powerful—besides making you objective!

In general, I think eye problems have much to do with a "point of view," a way of "looking" at things, and, in that sense, present a kind of blindness to other possibilities. Aside from the hypnotic cultural suggestion that eyes fail as we get older, I suspect poor eyesight is also reflecting a set in our prejudices or particular blindnesses. For instance, dyslexia (a condition in which the written word becomes jumbled) probably originates in a specific event which becomes a Stuck Picture (perhaps around the time when reading was being introduced at school). At the base of this Stuck Picture is a fear which the sufferer would rather be "blind to" than "look at."

*　*　*

I want to take up the nose separately because, while it has its association with the fifth chakrah and it is located nearest to the sixth chakrah, I suspect that the nose is a little outpost representing, symbolically, the self. I am told that olfactory messages go directly to the spinal column, rather than the brain as with other sensory messages. This, to my sense of logic, puts the nose under the domain of the first chakrah.

Our language is rich with allusions to the nose. We count noses, we are bidden to follow our noses and to keep them clean. Noses easily get out of joint. "I smell a rat," "Something stinks," "You're sweet," are all common expressions, mostly suggesting an association of the sense of smell with an evaluation of safety requirements. As the first chakrah holds sway over matters of physical safety as well as physical independence, I wonder if the nose doesn't represent the end of the line between the first chakrah and the top of the spinal column.

If we lose our sense of smell (our guide to safe passage?) because of a cold, are we expressing personal vulnerability in the face of in-dependence—an independence we may not want? Do we wish, because of this vulnerability, to be treated tenderly? Is a stuffy nose symbolic of congestion on the independence/dependence level?

*   *   *

The seventh chakrah is at the top of the head. It deals with intel-lectual information and psychic knowingness. People with high IQ's use this chakrah effectively. It is also the keeper of the analy-zer—the master computer where all our memories and beliefs are stored. In this context, consider the individual chakrahs as specific files under the domain of the master analyzer. The master analy-zer, in a very real sense, is the soul.

Because our beliefs define the self and are under the supervision of the seventh chakrah, this chakrah determines the degree of individualization or autonomy we are willing to experience or how bravely we wish to express our souls. Perhaps I can best ex-plain the seventh chakrah's domain of influence by saying that it is possible to cord to and from this chakrah. Any cord in this chakrah automatically puts the person so corded under the dominion of whatever the other end of the cord is attached to. Most cult mem-bers are corded on this level by their leaders. The cord can also come from a dominating spouse or parent or even a child. Psycho-logically, this manifests as extreme dependence upon following the lead of someone else. Someone else owns our soul. We have been "brainwashed" into accepting the belief systems of another as our own guides. A cord in this chakrah makes the owner of that chakrah a puppet. No one is corded on this level without his tacit consent. A cord on this level can also run to an abstract idea or "cause." Religious and political zealots have cords in this chakrah. They function from the belief systems handed to them by the group to which they belong. The price they have to pay is their own autonomy in matters which concern the self: they have lost dominion over their souls.

Possession, or the act of taking over a body by a discarnate entity, is achieved through this chakrah. The difference between cording and possession is really a matter of degree. Only those who feel they are weak in relation to a discarnate can be possessed by a discarnate. Only those who feel they are inadequate in their own right will permit or seek cording to someone or something else.

Headaches, generally, out-picture the pain of "wrong-headed-ness." The self may be caught between two beliefs which make effectiveness impossible—which makes autonomy impossible. When the headache goes away—you can't think constructively in the midst of pain—go back to the immediate onset of the head-ache and see if you can find two opposing directions which your beliefs are asking you to follow. Take responsibility for one direc-tion or the other. And take responsibility also for ignoring the directions you do not intend to follow. This will improve your chances of not getting the next headache. When following one direction at a time becomes a habit, these kinds of headaches should not occur. For myself, I find that one set of beliefs says I can't fulfill my own expectations and another set says I must. Is this what you are doing, too?

*　　*　　*

The feet have chakrahs too. They provide a connection be-tween the body and the earth. In that sense they reflect a commit-ment made to living in a *physical* body. We take bodies to have *physical* experiences—muscular, sexual, emotional, and sensuous experiences. Life should be rich in such expressions. Otherwise, we could just as easily function as timeless, spaceless mental points. If you are having foot or leg problems, you might ask yourself how committed you are to living in a physical dimension. Some of your ambivalence may have to do with a "life path" which is not to your liking. If you are on such an undesirable path, do you consider it stony? Uphill? Too difficult? Self-sacrificing? Crippling? Then ask yourself why you wish to pursue such a course when it makes life so unpleasant. Life should be joyous. Your feet or your legs may be telling you that you have chosen to make it otherwise.

*   *   *

The chakrahs in the palms of the hands sponsor one of our greatest resources. People who particularly enjoy working with their hands are using the creative/healing energy from these chakrahs to accomplish their goals. Artists, healers, gardeners, mechanics, tinkerers, musicians, a few doctors, and probably most nurses run this energy in large amounts. (I say "a few doctors" because medical schools favor other criteria for licensing.)

Many people carry blocks or prohibiting bands of energy at their wrists, stemming mostly, I believe, from a fear of free expression. If you have problem rashes, or your hands are perpetually cold or arthritic, consider what beliefs these symptoms might be expressing about your unwillingness to become involved in a full circle of giving and receiving generously. Are you trying to give more than you get—making someone else wrong for not giving?· Are you afraid of giving, lest you end up "short-handed?"

Sometimes the various fingers (and toes) are associated with chakrahs—the thumb with the first chakrah, the index finger with the second chakrah, etc. I'm not sure if this is appropriate or not. Yet, it may account for the gesture of raising the middle finger in an act of defiance or when we wish to assert the will of the self. In Western cultures, most wedding bands are worn on the third finger which would represent the heart chakrah. There is probably some validity behind these associations, but again, it may be oversimplified.

For diagnostic purposes, it can sometimes be helpful to know that one side of the body is characteristically the dominant side. It is usually the side of your hand preference. That is, for right-handed people, the right side would be the dominant side. Also for diagnostic purposes, it is helpful to think of psychic energy as being one of two types—male and female. Usually, *but not always,* the energy of your physical sex is associated with the dominant side of your body. A typical woman, for instance, would run female energy on her right side and male energy on her left side, though certainly such rules are made to be broken.

If you are having problems on one particular side—a shoulder, a hip, an arm perhaps—it might be profitable to look into whether or not you are uncomfortable with an aspect of your male/female duality. There is no sound reason, aside from cultural expectations, why men should not be predominantly intuitive, sensitive, and nurturing nor why women should not prefer to enjoy physical achievement and the use of authority. If you feel that it is not "feminine" to be forthrightly competitive or even intellectual, you *may* be attempting to subdue "the real you" by punishing the side which represents an aspect of yourself with which you do not feel comfortable.

To track down the cause of any set of physical symptoms, begin by listing all your symptoms individually, but not medically. For instance, don't say, "I have a cough," but say instead, "It hurts to breathe." Secondly, be dramatic. Don't merely say, "It hurts." Say, "It feels as if someone were standing on my chest." Does that analogy suggest to you that you have been conquered? What else comes to mind? Thirdly, try out all the commonly accepted turns-of-phrase which might apply to your symptom. A cough is considered to be a congestion of the lungs. What is it then which is causing you "congestion?" Or what are you trying to "cough up?" Get rid of? Our language is rich in these connections between figures of speech and physical symptoms. "She gives me a pain in the neck." "He's a yellow-livered coward." "You are breaking my heart." "There was a lump in my throat when I said good-bye."

Let's illustrate what I suggest by using that ache-all-over-feverish-misery-of-a-cold. Are your eyes watering? Puffy? Does that suggest tears to you? If you could cry, what would you cry about? Are you having difficulties breathing? Does this congestion come from being of two minds? Do you want to do something and not do something at the same time? What about the fever? Does that suggest anger? What are you so "hot" about? Do you feel nauseous? What, at a "gut level," is making you emotionally sick? Is there pain? To what emotional equivalent in your life do you relate that pain?

When you have done all of the above, you will have the emotional "look" of what is bothering you. It might read like this: "I want to cry because I feel so angry and hurt, but anger only makes things worse." (Remember the foot-on-the-chest symbolism? Did you stamp out a feeling?) "People should be nicer to me. I'm nice to them."

Note the organ or chakrah area where the symptom is manifesting. Can you gain any insights from the suggestions already given? All of these clues should remind you of something you *were* dealing with but chose to ignore and call settled. Applying the Three Day Rule to anything which comes up suddenly will almost invariably lead you directly to the incident with which you failed to cope adequately. (See Chapter 14.) This unresolved event is the source of your current problem. Sometimes you will find a series of events over a span of many days which, at first light, appear to have no connection with one another—an unpleasant phone call, difficulties on the job, a flat tire, etc.

Pick whichever event in the series has the greatest emotional impact for you. Work it through until you find the faulty belief. (See Chapter 14.) That belief will present you with the conclusion that you consider yourself impotent to act in your own behalf in the given situation. I repeat, you are not *really* impotent; you only play that game because you have set up your belief system incorrectly. (Again, see Chapter 14.)

The idea is that *if you do this process correctly,* you will get well a lot faster because you will have cleared up what is causing the symptom/event. In addition, the chances of having to manifest in this covert way again will be greatly reduced because some, if not all, of the cause for this particular behavior has been removed. You will also remove the base for far more serious consequences. Cancer, diabetes, etc., are conditions which are built up over long periods when root causes are ignored. In the case of cancer, for instance, it takes anywhere from 6 months to two years following a "life-threatening" emotional event for the symbolism to evince *as cancer.* What's more, the *originating* experience may have occurred many, many years before. Only last week I saw someone whose unsuccessful love affair was the specific event which created her cancer, but behind this was an unresolved emotional knot which arose from being sexually molested as a child. Yet all along the way, there had been plenty of evidence that a problem was building. The question is this: do you want to repair the leaks in your roof as you notice them, or do you want to wait until the entire roof caves in? One of the dreadful consequences of treating physical symptoms the way the medical profession does is that its solution is to put a small patch on the inside of the roof so that it *looks* as if there were no further problem. Yet all the while, the rotting roof goes unattended.

While we are discussing cancer, I think it fairly safe to say that, in the symbolism of the body, lump cancer suggests a specific event and systemic cancer (leukemia, for instance) may be of a more generalized character or a particular way of thinking. This is why paying attention to an accurate description of your symptoms is so important in the finding of true cause. The initiating event in both cases may have been a divorce, a death, the loss of a psychologically important job, a drastic change in a prime relationship, or even a profound "understanding" that you couldn't make your dreams come true.

Find that event and begin to deal with the still unresolved problems attached to it. Cancer can recur when it is treated by traditional methods because its true cause has not been resolved. Surgery, etc., may remove the *symptom* of the problem but not the cause. If traditional methods do effect a permanent cure, it is because either the event of having cancer or some new event has changed the patient's perspective. Thanks to his new found importance with his friends, his family, and with the medical profession, he is able to plug into a feeling of effectiveness. Cancer can also be eradicated because the patient has switched his attention from his divorce, for instance, to his life and death struggle with cancer. The divorce, then, gets put into a perspective which makes it relatively small and "manageable." Hence, there is no longer a need to manifest a symptom which is "unmanageable."

Cancer is said to be a disease which will affect 30% of the population. One reason we choose to express ourselves with cancer in such a high statistical frequency is that we have been programmed (given hypnotic suggestion) on a daily basis to fear its virulence. If doctors announced that they had found a simple (but actually worthless) pill which could immunize the population against cancer, our fears would vanish. Without such fear, perhaps 85% of those now falling prey to this constantly underscored fear, would no longer be victimized by the trap which we set for ourselves. Because we are reminded almost daily of how likely it is that we will get cancer, how dangerous it is, and how resistant to cure it is, the fear of cancer runs rampant. Our fear of cancer makes us vulnerable to cancer.

I once saw a film on the quest the Chinese had made to find out what was causing such a high incidence of esophageal cancer in a particular province. Because we live in the age of the chemical, and because the Chinese, unfortunately, now admire our scientific approach to problem solving, the team of investigators assumed that the people of this province were ingesting a carcinogen. Nothing they tested turned up anything even vaguely suggesting this was the case. Then they had the bright idea to isolate various chemicals within the various foods and combine them in such a way as to *construct* the end result they wanted—a carcinogen. Element A was found in the moldy bread (favored by the Chinese as we favor moldy cheese). Element B was found in what the pigs *ate* (though not apparently in their tissue!), etc. By carefully reconstructing the facts, they finally got the answer they had predetermined. Given that sort of gerrymandering, how many other diets could be demonstrated as carcinogenic?

The film editors interviewed three men who had been newly saved from the effects of esophageal cancer by modern science. They had had most of their throats removed. One man, to show how silly he had been in the days before such miracles had come to his province, said laughingly that it had been a popular belief throughout all the province that a family or personal problem was what caused cancer. His own family difficulties had been so great that his only son had left home. He admitted he had been silly enough to think that this incident had caused his cancer! He was, of course, properly grateful to the kind men who had cut out a portion of his throat for pointing out his mistakes.

Mind you, according to this man, the *entire province* believed as he believed—that personal problems create cancer. Even if that province and I are wrong in our belief that "great family difficulties" can, in fact, lead to cancer, if everyone believes in voodoo, then voodoo should certainly be investigated unless you intend to find only the "facts" you wish to find. Scientists do this consistently. That's okay—everyone with an opinion must do this, but scientists assure us that they alone *do not do this*. They assure us that they alone are impartial, objective, and interested only in abstract truth. This is a patent falsehood. They are as biased, subjective, and given to self-promotion as the rest of us. We do ourselves an inestimable disservice by not recognizing this fallacy in "scientific" information.

Before we end our discussions on physical symptoms I want to stress a point about pain that I have only mentioned in passing. Medically, pain can be one of the most elusive symptoms to treat effectively. There are even clinics which deal with nothing but this symptom. No matter what is said to be the physical cause of the pain—a slipped disc, pleuresy, a muscle spasm, etc.—I would look to an unresolved emotional pain as the creating cause of such discomfort. Emotions which are not put to rest *must* manifest in some way; there is no other alternative for that energy. Thus there is no true alternative but to deal with the creating cause if you would be rid of long term pain because doctors can't really help much.

Additionally I suspect that some pain arises from very deep causes, causes far deeper than mere ego games. I think of these causes as arising out of purpose or the will to live itself. In order to eradicate this kind of pain you may have to investigate the very roots of life as you construe that term. Has life been too hard? Are you mortally disappointed? It would be my hope that this book has given you sufficient spiritual information to begin to address this problem too.

The purpose of this chapter has been to introduce you to a new way of thinking about your symptoms. I hope you use it only as a springboard to stimulate your own imagination. If your own intuition takes you in a different direction than mine, by all means, follow your own lead. For instance, an artist friend of mine has been going through a series of serious eye problems. *For her,* her eyes represent herself. They are absolutely indispensable to a description of "who she is." The questions she asks about the cause of her eye problems should address themselves, therefore, to what her eyes mean to her and her self, not necessarily to what I have to say in such general terms. Be guided then by your own inner knowingness, not a textbook simplification.

17.

How To Heal

W E EFFECT HEALINGS by exchanging a set of negative beliefs for a set of positive beliefs. It's as simple as that. The difficulty in effecting such a transformation comes from our resistance to giving up a cherished and meaningful negative belief in favor of an untested positive one.

This book has attempted to persuade you that such a procedure is both logically feasible and eminently rewarding, but in the final analysis, it is only you who can prove this to yourself. If you would like to bring miracles into your life by healing your circumstances, then I suggest you start by first using the steps given below in small ways. You have no idea what a boost it is to "heal" for something as minor as finding a parking place in the right spot and then having it appear. "My God! This really works!!" is likely to be your response. "If I can do this, what else can I do?"

Build on your success with any small event you can think of— "Someone will call today and suggest a movie." "Everyone I meet today will be particularly pleasant." "When I wake up tomorrow morning, my sore throat will be gone." These healings should anticipate occasions which are just beyond your normal expectations so that when they happen you cannot logically attribute them to "what would have happened anyway," but not so far beyond them that they seriously challenge your credulity that such an event is possible.

Give yourself tasks which are increasingly more adventure-some. It is not a matter of finding where the system breaks down. It can't. It is your faith in possibility which breaks down. If you could bring yourself to *know* that a million dollars would float through the window and land in a litter at your feet, this is exactly what would *have* to happen. It is *only* your belief that this can't happen which makes it impossible. The system is constructed in such a way that it will only keep pace with your expectations. Your effort, therefore, must go to increasing those expectations in measured steps.

The first and only difficult step is substituting a belief in what appears to be so implacably real for another belief which makes the opposite possibility even more real. When I effected my first "big" healing, it took considerable determination to overcome this stumbling block. Because I worked at it so doggedly and be-cause it proved to be so successful, I give you my experience as an instructive example for a beginner.

What I wanted was money. I was in debt, I had five children to feed, and every day was a discouraging struggle. At the time, I was a real estate agent working on commission. This meant that money came to me in big chunks or it didn't come at all—a feast or famine arrangement which I found nerve-wracking. What I determined to heal into existence was a sum of money equal to half my yearly income and I wanted it in six days. Incidentally, there is no difference in the techniques used in healing for money (or any other circumstances) than those used in healing for health. I call all such events healings because they cure a negative circum-stance. I am using a healing for circumstance as an example be-cause all the action is external. We can watch what is happening. When a healing occurs in a body, all the action is internal and we cannot watch it. We can only see the end result.

I made no stipulation as to *how* the money would come to me. A check in the mail would have been entirely acceptable! This is im-portant. In making healings for the body, we do not ask that the blood perform in a particular way or that the liver increase the production of a specific chemical because we do not now enough to be sure such adjustments will accomplish the result we desire. When we heal, we should envision *end results,* not the intermediate steps. In the same way, we reach for a pencil, confident that the intermediate steps—which we could not properly detail in any case—will be accomplished correctly.

I was very specific about exactly what I wanted. I had an exact dollar amount and an exact time limit. If I had said, "I know things will get better for me financially," they would have, had I been able to confidently hold that thought. This would have been one way to solve the problem. But we are speaking of miracles—events which are not otherwise to be credited. Moreover, in terms of "proof" that the system works, the slower process can easily be attributed mistakenly to a variety of causes. A doubting pragmatist might easily overlook the link between mental action and outcome.

In order to switch my beliefs from nearly a lifetime of penny-pinching and fear that there would never be enough money, I pretended that beliefs and the directions they represented looked like a wool pompom—strands of yarn tied at the center and extending outward in all directions. Why was one strand more precious than any other, I asked myself? Wasn't I free to choose whichever strand I wished? Whenever I became bogged down with what I believed and didn't believe, I returned to this imagery to help me get over the notion that one belief had any more reality than another.

I spent a good deal of time imagining that the event had already happened. I imagined having the money in my hand. How did that feel? I was excited by my success, relieved and relaxed because I had the money and didn't have to worry anymore. I fairly wallowed in the expanse of such a fantasy. *I made it real.* When I had enjoyed the scene in all its pleasure, I then asked myself if I thought such a scene possible. The answer was yes, *but . . .* and the *but* told me I wasn't ready.

Back I went to the drawing board. Once again I supported my intellectual belief that the healing *should* happen with every argument I could think of. I assured myself that my precarious financial position was due solely to a belief in that kind of reality. I brought to earth every reason I could find for why a healing wouldn't work, and I looked at all those "reasons" with the idea of releasing my doubt. I practiced making the anticipated future a present event in my imagination by positive argument. "As you believe, so shall it appear," was a phrase I constantly repeated. Did I believe that statement? Well then?

Eventually—and this first attempt took me some weeks of effort—something clicked over in my mind. From a place beyond doubt, I came at last to know that this event would happen.

At this point I slipped effortlessly into a state of mind I can best describe as objective curiosity. My only thought was *how* it was all going to come about, but I never questioned *if* it were going to happen. I think one test of whether or not you have truly succeeded in transferring your trust to the desired end is achieving this calm knowingness. If you are anxious, it is an expression of doubt. Doubt only produces a mirroring of those doubts—doubtful results. Every part of your mind must KNOW and if it does, there can be no other possible emotional reaction but peace.

I was up early the next morning, determined to do my part in this great adventure by going to the office and looking up every house on the market if that was what it took. I was about an hour into this project when I said, "Hey, wait a minute. This effort is saying, 'Barbara, unless you do something extraordinary this miracle is not going to happen.' What would you do if you KNEW it would happen?" The answer was that I would go home and do the laundry. And this was just what I did. And indeed, it wasn't long before the phone rang there. It was a client reconsidering a house I had suggested to her some time before. Now, "suddenly" she wanted to see it. And I knew she would buy it.

I have never worked so hard as I did in those next few days. But I never made work. I took my lead naturally from others. I followed each step to the very best of my ability but in a strange way I never took control. Rather, I allowed myself to be led. In that sense I was borne along on currents to which I was ever responsive but never tried seriously to direct. For example, about 8 hours before the deadline I found myself arguing (politely and because of my fatigue) against showing a house until this particular couple returned from a long weekend. I hadn't made my goal but I had come close and those people had been looking for years. Politeness prevailed (as did the current I am trying to describe) and to make a long story short, by a few minutes before midnight (my witching hour) I had achieved my goal and then some. The offer was presented to the seller at 11 p.m. She was leaving permanently for New York at some frightful hour like 2 a.m. and was as eager for this odd business hour as I. This is one of the beauties in doing things this way. Everyone's wishes dovetail so perfectly.

That week was filled with such strange coincidences. One couple who called had picked up an old newspaper listing a house which I had all but given up on and was not currently advertising. They called the office at 8 in the evening and my broker "just happened" to be there and "just happened" to pick up the phone instead of letting the answering service catch it. The couple explained later that under usual conditions, they would have waited until morning and called the agent with whom they had been working, but on a "sudden impulse" they had decided to follow through on their own. I felt sorry for that agent. I knew he or she was holding thoughts very like my own of the previous week. I showed the house at 9 p.m. and I knew I had it sold even before I met them.

One of my clients was a doctor. I needed his signature on a series of counter-offers but no one at the hospital to which I had tracked him knew how to find him as he hadn't answered his page for some hours. "Well, he'll just have to come to me," I said, as I settled myself to wait where I could glimpse an intersecting corridor. Within a few minutes he walked right down that corridor and I ran after him to get the papers signed.

At the height of all this feverish activity, I got a bladder infection. "I can't stop for this," I groaned. And yet it is hard being business-like when you must go to the bathroom every 3 or 4 minutes. "Well . . . why not heal this, too?" I asked myself. And so I did—in a matter of minutes all symptoms were gone. One seller unexpectedly returned from an extended trip and more unexpectedly was now willing to carry a second mortgage although he had previously declared that such an arrangement was out of the question.

As a matter of fact, the entire week was filled with one big surprise after another. The only thing which wasn't surprising was the end result. No, that was surprising, too! I exceeded my goal by 10%. Few, if any, of these deals were easy to negotiate. There was an extra lot with one house which had to be patiently dealt with, back and forth. One seller was particularly difficult. She is best described by the fact that she took every light bulb and toilet paper spindle with her when she left the house. All deals involved special financing problems, but new and innovative ideas on how to solve each of these problems just seemed to swim into my mind.

Here again, I must emphasize the distinction between "not taking the lead" and making no contribution. I saw myself as a willing problem solver, engaging my energies in finding a solution whenever a snag arose, but I didn't feel compelled to take any initiative beyond what would be considered my normal work habits. In other words, I cooperated full-heartedly with the operating force in every way I could, but I never tried to create my own force beyond the original healing I had set in motion. I trusted the healing force to guide me correctly using my natural patterns of behavior as one of the elements it would work with. As they say in Alcoholics Anonymous, I "let go and let God."

*   *   *

Since that time I have effected many miracles, both for myself and for others. The miracle I would most like to effect now is for you. I would like to lift every burden from your shoulders. I truly would, for I have small tolerance for the suffering of others. But I can't. And that's good. If I could impose my wishes on you, you would no longer possess your soul. I would. The Creating Cosmos forbids such interference with your freedom by making you supreme in your own universe—even if you don't wish to be! The most I can do is point a path because it really is a me-AND-you world.

To that end, I give you this new concept of the Creating Cosmos. If you accept it, you will be enormously rewarded. You need no longer embrace the popular religious view of yourself as a sinner. You need no longer accept the scientific assessment of your worth—an assessment which all but pushes you off the cosmic stage. Instead you can claim your rightful heritage as the powerful center of your own universe. You may count yourself divine. You may take comfort in your immortality. You may draw strength from your knowledge that you are one with the mothering source of the universe. I do not think it an accident that we are physically conceived within the nurturing protection of a mother. This is but the outward symbolism of the larger truth of our existence.

Freed from doubts as to your worth and origins, you may turn your attention to endeavors which truly do produce happiness— the full expression of a love of self in harmonious affection for All That Is. Life need not be the confrontational challenge of fear. It can be an experiment in cooperation and love. The Creating Cosmos gives you the freedom of such a choice secured by the promise that life will be as you believe.

Desiderata

May you love generously without trading it for love returned.

May your life always enhance the lives of others.

May you allow others to be right for themselves.

May you continuously break down the barriers of self-imposed limitations.

May you feel your indivisible involvement with all aspects of the universe and may your joy in this be part of your everyday experience.

May you commit yourself enthusiastically to all you do.

May you understand that you cannot find yourself except through action, you cannot find love except through your own lovingness, and you cannot find happiness except as you step beyond yourself to become deeply involved with others.

May you rest in peace, knowing you are the center of power in your own universe.

Index

Acquired Immune Deficiency
  Syndrome (AIDS), 162
Akashic Records, 18, 19
Analyzer (of mind), 43, 49–50
Anticipation, importance of, 145
"As thou hast believeth". . ., 55
Asthma, 169
Astral travel, 13, 166
Atherosclerosis, 162
Autism, 158

Beliefs, 34, 42–53
  as guidance system, 44, 51
Berkeley Psychic Institute, 79
Bi-location, 14
Bladder, 161
Blaming, 91
Blood pressure, 162, 167
Breakthrough to Creativity, 19
Bostwick, Lewis, 79
Bowels, 161
Brain, 31
  as computer, 5, 15
Breatharianism, 16, 146

Calories, 150
Cancer, 25, 28, 169, 177–179
Capote, Truman, 20
Casteneda, Carlos, 17, 20
Cause, in search of, 120–133
Cayce, Edgar, 22, 59, 146, 149
Central nervous system, 158
Chakrahs, 74, 153–174
  description of, 153–156
  1st (survival), 157
  2nd (emotional/sexual), 161
  3rd (energy), 164
  4th (heart), 167
  5th (communication), 168
  6th (clairvoyance), 170
  7th (knowingness), 172
  feet, 173
  hands, 174
Cholesterol, 148, 162, 167
Clairsentience, 24
Clairvoyance, 23
Colds, as symbols, 61
Creating Cosmos, 3, 4–10, 34,
  35, 72, 187
  definition of, 6

Creating Cosmos, The, 4, 54
Creating Creations, 67–69
Critical mass (of energy/intention), 7, 36
Culture, in transition, 38–40

Da Vinci, Leonardo, 22
Decisions produce personal history, 46
Dental/oral problems, 169
Dependency, and 1st chakra, 158
Diabetes, 165
Disease, definition of, 135
Divine, definition of, 6
Doctors as advisors, 141
Dowsing, 27
Dream Time, 67
Dyslexia, 171

Ears, 168
Edema, 161
Effectiveness, personal, 38
Effort equated with purpose, 40
Ego, 45, 81–87
Emotion, 36
  as psychic energy, 70–71
Emotions, negative, 101–110
  anger, 107
  anxiety, 110
  envy, 106
  grief, 102
  guilt, 104
  hate, 109
  jealousy, 105
  self-pity, 101
Emphysema, 169
Endocrine system, 170

Endorphines, 163
Endosphere, definition of, 5
Energy, bands of 17; female/male, 175
Energy, psychic, *See* psychic energy
Environment, creation of, 59
Exorcism, 21
Eyes, 171

Fear, 47, 92, 118
  expressed in negative emotions, 101–111
  facing _____, 118
  expressed at chakrah level, 157–174
Feet, 173
Findhorn Community, 19
Fingers, 174

Gandhi, 84, 85
Gastro-intestinal system, 164, 165
Good, externalized as God, 12
Gorillas, 37

Hands, 174
Headaches, 173
Heal, how to, 181–188
Healings, 2, 27–29
Health, 114, 144, 151
  beliefs about _____, 134–151
  body's healing power, 139
  the environment of _____, 143
Heart, 167
Higher Sense Perception, 19
Holmes, Ernest, 1
Hormones, 170

Hospitals, 142
Hypnotic suggestion of beliefs, 138
Hypnotism, 56–57
Hypoglycemia, 165
I-ams, 7, 8, 13, 54, 59
Immortality, 5
Immune system, 161, 162
Instincts, 42

Jesus, 13, 55

Karagulla, Shafica, 19, 20
Kidneys, 161
King, Jr., Martin Luther, 85
Kirlian photography, 73
Kissing the snake, 118

Larkrise to Candleford, 136
Laws of Mind, 56–62
Levitation, 14
Liver, 161, 162
Love, 97, 106
Lower back pain, 158–160
Lymphatic system, 161

Me-AND-you, 83, 115
Medicine, allopathic, 148
Me-OR-you, 83, 115
Metabolic system, 164, 165
Mind, 2, 5, 13
    imagination is real to____, 56
    as spaceless condition, 57–59
    as timeless condition, 59–61
    as programmer, 63–67
    as creating agent, 54–69
    See also psychic energy
"Mind over matter," 25–28

Miracles, 65
Mouth, 168

Nervous disorders, 160
Nose, 168, 171

Old Age, 17
Other people, role of, 82, 90

Pain, 163, 180
Parkinson's Disease, 160
Penicillin, effect of, 149
Photographic memories, 20
Photography, psychic, 25
Pneumonia, 169
Poltergeist, 14
Power, of humans, 6, 32, 115
Powers of the Mind, 11–32
Prime Creative Act, 5
Psychics, 23
Psychic energy, 5
    management of 7, 33–36, 55
    utilization of to out-picture
        thought, 60–61
    as emotion, 70
    within chakrahs, 153–156
    cords, 158, 165, 169, 172
    See also Mind
Psychic Energy Field (aura),
    73–80
    as protection, 76
    as storage bin, 77
Psychic Surgery, 29
Psychometry, 23
Purpose of life, 8–9, 37–41
Pyramids, 15

Reading Dynamics, 21
Reality, rings of, 115–118
Respiratory system, 168, 169
Right/wrong game, 88–100
    losing the_____, 101–111
    destructive of the good life, 113
Rights, self assigned, 112
Roberts, Jane, 22

Schooling, as indoctrination, 46
Science of Mind, 1
Self-destructiveness, 90
Self-hood, 7, 8
Self-reliance/sufficiency,
    113–114
Seth, 22
Sex organs, 162
Skin problems, 76
Spine, 160
Spleen, 161, 162
Stalin, Joseph, 30
Stonehenge, 15
Stuck Pictures, 98–100, 120–130
    in auras, 78–79
Survival purpose, 83–87
Symbolism, in physical reality,
    61

Taking responsibility, 92, 104
Theory of Laminated Spacetime,
    The, 4
Thompson, Flora, 136
Thought, language of, 61
Throat, 168
Three Day Rule, 127
Transcendent purpose, 83–87,
    115
Transmediumism, 21–22
Transmutation of food, 147

Validation, 97
Vascular system, 162, 167, 168
Victim, playing the role of, 92,
    93, 94–95, 112
    women as—, 93–94
Vitamin C, 147

Walking on coals, 16
War, creation of, 60
    as right/wrong game, 89
Weight problems, 165
Welfare safety nets, 40
Will to live, 34
Wipe Out Pictures, 122, 130
Women as victims, 93–94
Wrong Action, defense of, 90

Yogis, 15

Colophon

This book was designed by Michael Sykes and the author. It was typeset in Baskerville and produced by Michael Sykes, printed on acid-free paper and bound by Braun-Brumfield, Inc. in the Spring of 1985. The display type was composed by David Bunnett and the dust jacket was designed by the author. The illustrations are by the author.

The Theory of Laminated Spacetime   **Barbara Dewey**

The Theory of Laminated Spacetime (dis-continuous time) is surely the most revolutionary and far-reaching proposal ever suggested in the name of science. Not only does Dewey address the difficult subject of physics with a layman's good-humored clarity, but by extending the theory's physical implications she has discovered *the causes* of such phenomena as gravity, magnetism, polarity, elliptical orbits, electron shells, etc. Indeed, so many physical anomolies have been solved that the theory must inevitably be taken for fact. The book is therefore a must-read for every physicist and layman who has ever been curious about the laws under which the physical universe functions.

Hardcover, 116 pages, 31 diagrams   **$16.95 postpaid**

The Creating Cosmos   **Barbara Dewey**

Dewey's Theory of Laminated Spacetime is explored from the spiritual/humanistic point of view. Again, the theory may well be the single most important intellectual contribution ever offered in the name of understanding our universe, its purposes and origins, and its laws of cause and effect. With lively good humor the author examines contemporary truths concerning God and man and then goes on to offer a different truth. It is a truth which makes each of us "divine" creators in a cosmos where the act of creation itself is the sponsoring power. The book is for everyone who has ever wondered about the purpose of life, the God-concept, and the path to spiritual attunement.

Hardcover, 128 pages   **$16.95 postpaid**

As You Believe   **Barbara Dewey**

Because life itself is supported by the creating power of mind, each of us unavoidably produces the events of our lives. Knowing this we can now choose those events consciously. This is a practical how-to book for those who wish to stop pulling disasters into their lives. From cancer to money problems, from distressing job situations to unhappy love affairs, *As You Believe* presents a radically new and proven approach to personal problem solving. Based on the author's many years of experience as a psychic reader/healer, the book explains the inner processes which convert beliefs into events, details how to find the beliefs which are causing negative experiences, and then describes exactly how to effectively heal for positive "miracles."

Hardcover, 208 pages   **$18.95 postpaid**

Order Form

Please send me the following books postpaid: Total

_____ Copies of *The Creating Cosmos* @ $16.95 each _____

_____ Copies of *The Theory of Laminated Spacetime*
@ $16.95 each _____

_____ Copies of *As You Believe* @ $18.95 each _____

Californians: Please add 6% sales tax _____

Grand Total: _____

Name: _____

Address: _____

_____ Zip: _____

Send to:

**Bartholomew Books
Box 634
Inverness, CA 94937
(415) 669-1664**